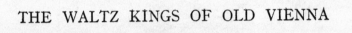
THE WALTZ KINGS OF OLD VIENNA

JOHANN STRAUSS, VATER.

THE WALTZ KINGS OF OLD VIENNA

By

ADA B. TEETGEN

With a Preface by

BECKET WILLIAMS

BOOKS FOR LIBRARIES PRESS
FREEPORT, NEW YORK

First Published 1939
Reprinted 1970

STANDARD BOOK NUMBER:
8369-5198-0

LIBRARY OF CONGRESS CATALOG CARD NUMBER:
78-107833

TO
LUISE AND JOSEF

PREFACE

THIS is to introduce a very entertaining book. It is certainly about time that it was written, and the history of the Strausses made available in English. What a pair they were, and what a period they lived in! The whole glamour that encircles musicians, even nowadays, probably started from Vienna in the 'forties and 'fifties. The long curly-haired gypsy type of the Romances, with melting eyes and throbbing fiddle, was surely founded on the Waltz Kings. The consumptive Chopin is now a trifle *démodé*, and the unsophisticated never took kindly to the burly Handel or irritable Beethoven. Even Mendelssohn with his cloak and luscious side-whiskers failed to wield the power of the Viennese or Hungarian Romany. The hypnotic spell of the Strausses affected even the learned. We read that Wagner (certainly aged only 19, but still Wagner), rhapsodised over their playing and milieu. Among dozens more, Berlioz and Brahms were captivated too.

The author of this book has been very well advised to paint so picturesquely the background of the period, for it is most essential to understand the hectic times in which the composers lived. Plutarch lays it down that a comfortable nation is hard to govern, but distressed peoples are easy to rule. Perhaps this may account for the extraordinary influence that the Strausses commanded. The worried Austrians would spend their last shilling on a restaurant where they were playing. Things were much the same after the last War, as I can testify myself, for

I was in Vienna at the time. And, indeed, so it was in England during the War itself, though the parallel is not quite correct, because money was then plentiful. The theatres and dance-halls were crowded, and the ubiquitous night-clubs began to arise.

Certain it was that the time made the men, in the case of the Strausses, as in most others.

Reading through these pages about past times, we may frequently imagine ourselves in the present. The younger Strauss was worked to death, like any Jazz-band leader to-day. Frequently he had to appear at five or more places in the same evening. Such a life, without trains and motors to transport them, may well make members of our "gig-bands" pause in horror.

Again, we could apparently teach the Viennese of that time little of the value and technique of publicity. Nor was the bad taste of to-day absent, as instanced by wretched bandmasters "jazzing" the classics, for we read that Rossini's "Stabat Mater" was made into a set of Quadrilles! Then, as now, there was the eternal difficulty about librettists, and there seem to have been hosts of "ghosts" who put them into shape, orchestrated them, and arranged them.

But there were differences. Johann senior, though an execrable contrapuntist, had to compose a "Gradual" (to the uninitiated, part of the Mass), before the authorities allowed him to conduct an orchestra. How I would love to make Mr. Jack Hylton write a "Credo"!

But the great difference is that there seems to be no one capable of writing a "Blue Danube" now, or any piece of dance music that outlives the year. . . .

Besides the Strausses, other names well-known to wireless enthusiasts occur over and over again in these pages.

Von Suppé, whose "Poet and Peasant" Overture seems

to me as trite and vulgar, as his "Light Cavalry" is good.
Offenbach, too, the composer of the hackneyed "Barcarolle"
and the delicious "Orpheus in the Underworld." As a
technician Offenbach was superior to either of the Strausses,
but he lacked their intense melodic energy. He pictures
Paris of the Empire, and the Strausses picture Vienna.
Perhaps that is their difference.

The abundant fertility of both father and son had its
disadvantages. Many of their works show signs of that
haste which is inseparable from their sort of existence.
Very much of it is frankly dull to us nowadays (especially
does this criticism apply to the father's). But we have
the "Tales from the Vienna Woods", "Die Fledermaus"
and "The Blue Danube", so let us be thankful.

My memories of "The Blue Danube" go back thirty
years or so, when my elder sister used to attack it with
gusto, on our silk-bosomed piano. Her performance was
not guided by strict accuracy, but the waltz opened a world
of beauty to me. Then, from 1913 to about 1930, I practically never heard it in England. Why was this? Was it
some stupidity about the War? Surely not. I think what
happened was that the denizens of "Tin-Pan Alley" were
wise enough to shelve a work that would show them up so
badly.

But you cannot keep a good man down, or a good tune
asleep, and now it has become as popular as ever. And
here may I mention that it is always taken too slowly over
here? In Vienna it is played at a brisk *tempo*, almost twice
as fast, and it is much more exhilarating. Whether it was
"dramatised" in the days of its composer, as it is now by
certain "hot" bands, I do not know. I can quite imagine it
was, for Strauss *fils* seemed to lack nothing in showmanship.

The author quotes Ernst Decsey's stimulating question
as to what would have happened if Strauss had had Brahms'

profound musicianship, or Brahms had had the former's fertile melodic sense. I think the answer is—nothing. Strauss would have been so hampered by a scholarly technique that he would have written but a fraction of what he did, and Brahms would have been ashamed of most of Strauss' thematic material. But it is an interesting question.

Finally, I will quote from the erratic Berlioz. He wrote, in the famous Memoirs, about Strauss the younger as follows:

"Strauss is an artist. The influence he has already exercised over musical feeling throughout Europe in introducing cross rhythms into waltzes is not sufficiently appreciated. So piquant is the effect, that the dancers themselves have already sought to imitate it by creating the *deux temps* waltz, although the music itself has kept the triple rhythm. If, out of Germany, the public at large can be induced to understand the singular charm frequently resulting from contrary rhythms it will be entirely owing to Strauss. Beethoven's marvels in this style are too far above it, and act at present only upon exceptional hearers. Strauss has addressed himself to the masses, and his numerous imitators have been forced to second him.

"The simultaneous employment of the various divisions of the bar, and syncopated accentuation of the tune, even in a regular and invariable form, is to simple rhythm what the harmonies of moving parts are to plain chords; I might even say, what harmony is to unison."

So the Jazz-fiends have discovered nothing fresh, as we knew.

BECKET WILLIAMS.

St. John's Wood,
  New Year, 1939.

FOREWORD

Although so much less than justice has been done to the two Strausses in English musical biography, there is, of course, a Strauss literature in German. The present work does not pretend to have of itself either original or musically critical merit. Based as it has necessarily been upon a study of the serious exponents of Strauss (as well as upon the handful of charming and sometimes very Viennese romances turning on their lives), it has no greater ambition than to address itself to the wireless listener who will always make a mark on the programme against the Overture to "Fledermaus". Its object has been rather to tell a story than to present a study.

Those who would wish to make a serious study of Strauss the musician, father or son, should address themselves to the works of Herr Fritz Lange, than which nothing can be more exhaustive or more romantically interesting, and also to the important critical study of the Strausses more recently contributed to their literature by Herr Ernst Decsey.

The present writer chiefly owes what worth and interest her book may have to these authorities. Without these, of course, it could not have been written.

Among the works of Herr Lange she would mention his *Johann Strauss*, the thirty-first volume of a series of small musical biographies published by the Firma Phillipp Reclam Jun. in Leipzig.

Next she would put Herr Decsey's monumental study *Johann Strauss: Ein Wiener Buch*, published in Berlin by the Verlag Hesse. She takes this opportunity of thanking cordially both Houses for their permission to make what use she has of their works, and to quote from them. She also has to make sincere acknowledgements to the publishers of "Des Walzerkönigs Liebestraum", by Herr R. Kleinecke, Messrs. Ensslin and Laiblins of Reutlingen, for permission to derive some very picturesque details from these pages.

In writing a book of this description the author is necessarily indebted to more sources for information and for colour than it would be easy to ennumerate, or indeed specifically to acknowledge, especially when her use of her authority has been so wide of any literal quotation that it was not really practical to signalise the passage. She has, however, to thank Messrs. Harper Brothers for kindly allowing her to quote from Madame Lindencrone's *In the Courts of Memory;* and Messrs. Macmillan for similar permissions with regard to Mr. Crankshaw's *Vienna,* and Mr. Redlich's *Emperor Francis Joseph of Austria.*

With regard to passages taken from the English version of *The Bat* (Ch. xv) the author can only say that she wrote to the publishers in Vienna on the matter, but received no reply. As the reason for this may possibly be surmised, she ventures to retain her quotations, and offers grateful acknowledgements for them—as indeed for all others—in this place.

She is indebted to Herr Dr. Katann, Director of the Historical Museum in Vienna for his very kind assistance in procuring for her the illustrations, and to the friend who photographed the Strauss monuments especially for this book. She would also thank H. E. Hill, Esq. and literary friends abroad for much encouragement and many good offices in connection with it.

ADA B. TEETGEN.

CONTENTS

LIST OF ILLUSTRATIONS

THE WALTZ KINGS OF OLD VIENNA

CHAPTER I

THE HABSBURG A.E.I.O.U.
ALLES ERDREICH IST OESTERREICH UNTERTHAN
OR
AUSTRIAE EST IMPERARE ORBI UNIVERSO

IT is a curious thing that no account of the two Johann Strausses, father and son, has as yet appeared in English; that no volume on the "Waltz King" and his glittering period is to be found in any library of musical biography.

Johann Strauss, whether father or son (and the Strauss legend from beginning to end was one), yet retains a place almost daily in our Radio programmes despite the popularity of far more modern dance music. Whether the waltz itself will ever give place entirely to dance rhythms which would certainly have amazed the writer of the "Frühlingswalzer", is a companion question as to whether jazz, highbrow or low-brow, will wholly relegate the dance music of the nineteenth century to limbo. Many people, no doubt, still exist who hope it will not. A Strauss waltz is a thing which does not lose its charm. That the two Viennese wizards of the baton and the bow (to say nothing of the *four*—including Josef and Eduard), are now represented, in England at least, by a mere score of their dance compositions and a couple of operettas at the most, argues little against the claim of some of the most prolific, melodious and enchanting "Komponisten" to a niche in the temple of fame.

No one, of course, would compare them with the giants. To criticise the Strausses, Johann the second in particular, as musicians of little account in comparison with that galaxy of masters who immediately preceded them in Vienna, and of those who were contemporaneous with them elsewhere in Europe, is entirely superfluous. Everyone knows that Schubert could have written any one of Johann's works if he had wished, but that Johann could not have written Schubert's. The point need really not be stressed when it is remembered that popular music, the music of the entertainer, must never be judged by classical standards, the standards of the creators, the thinkers, (although Wagner once said of Strauss: "He has the most musical head in Europe . . . long live our classicists from Mozart to Strauss." Wagner often played Strauss music).

Nevertheless the Strausses, father *or* eldest son, were more than bandmasters, inspired scribblers of waltzes, servants or idols of gay and fashionable society given up to pleasure. That they have been recognised for far more than this, abroad, is evident not only from the serious historical, analytical, musical literature which has grown up about them in German, but also from the apology which was made in 1922 for the appearance of yet another book on the subject. Strauss the younger died in 1899. The life work of this artist was worthy of a fresh review from a longer perspective. It was then seen to have derived directly and most picturesquely from nature, from the Donau and Wiener Wald—from the beautiful valley of the Danube, and the wooded country around Vienna—as also from a sound and healthy tradition of folk song and dance. In its genesis it was pure, and of a sturdy worth, and it ended in a philosophy and a mission which may indeed have a vital interest even for us to-day.

It lent itself, as it came to conquer the capital of one of the most heterogeneous Empires the world has ever seen, to a purpose and an interpretation which cannot perhaps be claimed for any of the music of our own confused, disunited, inharmonious world.

An old Viennese Court official used to say that the Emperor Franz Josef just lived on Strauss to his dying day. When the Idol of Vienna died, there went also half the old light-hearted politically-ramshackle Austria which the Kaiser had held together only with so much difficulty. With the collapse of the Dual Monarchy, at the end of the Great War, "the last smile vanished from the face of a society to which Raimund, Lanner, and Strauss had taught a veritable intoxication of gaiety."

The Viennese are naturally a light-hearted, gentle-minded, happy people, and they remain so to-day, largely thanks to the influence of Johann Strauss, despite the fearful troubles through which the city and the country have passed during the last disastrous years. He stands, a golden figure, with his still bewitching violin uplifted in the sunlight, in one of the green gardens of Vienna to-day, and whenever the first bars of a Strauss melody strike up, expatriated Austrians both smile and weep.[1]

In 1848 Franz Josef as quite a young man, newly come to the Habsburg throne, chose for his country a Latin motto which never worked out so harmoniously as in the waltz Strauss wrote under the same name, "Viribus Unitis". This motto indeed was far better suited to the life work of the composer than to that of the highly unconstitutionally-minded autocrat who originally chose it. Austria was never a nation in the racial signification of the term,

[1] This was written just prior to the Anschluss, March '38.

but rather a conglomeration of mutually antipathetic peoples. The same racial antipathies constitute one of the most knotty problems of central Europe to-day. The only conciliatory voice to uplift itself in nineteenth century Vienna, was that of Strauss's wonder violin, whose musical pleadings did more to unite the disunited, to appease animosities, and to dissolve inter-racial strife—in the carefree delight of the dance—than all the questionable efforts of the nobility and of the politicians put together.

Strauss, says Ernst Decsey, one of his most serious exponents, "founded a rhythmical League of Nations". His appeal to the peoples of the Dual Empire in his time was wholly successful as far as it went. It had the same sort of appeal as international sport may have to-day. It both mitigated asperities, and promoted cordialities. If the awkward amalgam that was Austria-Hungary under Franz Josef produced anything in common, it produced Strauss's music.

"The Blue Danube" was, and remains perhaps, for that country, what "Finlandia" is for the Finn, the "Marseillaise" for France, and "Land of Hope and Glory" for us. When conferences and pacts, when treaties and leagues, break down, there remain two things which may still help the cause of international understanding in Europe—music and sport. Strauss defended and promoted it with dance tunes throughout the nineteenth century, and for this alone he should mean more to the Radio listener to-day than merely a hackneyed name to a hackneyed melody.

He was a significant figure through a significant period. Something of special interest attaches to every one of his multitudinous compositions, and to the occasions which gave rise to them.

Latterly his Austria dwindled away to nothing. Sir

Philip Gibbs described the country a few years ago as "a head without a body"! Nevertheless, in all her post-war poverty Vienna still possesses Schubert, Lanner, Raimund, Strauss. Only recently a great ball was held commemorative of the last, in which the ballroom was made to recall a famous "Tanz Lokal" of the past, and in which the dancers wore the costumes of two generations ago. Someone once wrote that what the Napoleonic victories remain to France, the Strauss tradition still remains to Vienna. Strauss père and then Strauss fils conquered the world of their day, not with the Marshal's baton, but with the fiddle-bow.

The art of the Strausses, father and son, remained ever popular, deriving directly from its source among the folk, and preserved the ring of truth to nature even to the last.

Nature herself, indeed, breathes through all their work. The twittering of the village sparrow is heard in many a light and birdlike passage, and now and then the lapping of the river breaks into the most classic of the Viennese waltzes. The trilling and jodelling of the green-clad Alpine villagers echo later in the ballrooms of the Royal and Imperial Court.

It has been said that the chief characteristics of the Viennese in general can be attributed to the charm of the Danube landscape.[1] It is a sort of musical optimism, unlike anything else, and expresses a realisation of the gifts of Life, Dance, Song and Love. Its music is the music of universal happiness.

The Strausses' fame rests largely on their waltzes, because waltzes were what their profession and position exacted of them, and what their public incessantly demanded with ever increasing clamour, and often at the shortest notice. Both father and son, however, achieved more important work.

---

[1] "Landschaft," sagt Lissauer, "ist ein Zustand der Seele." Landscape is an attitude of the spirit.

Unlike the majority of famous musicians, and unlike his father, Johann Strauss, the son, had a happy and successful life. He belongs to that infinitely remote period—now—which, despite a thousand sneers, seems to have been stable, prosperous, and secure, compared to the thin times the world has been passing through since. His life fills a crowded and brilliant page in the story of that day; without the strains of his music the reconstruction of any nineteenth-century ballroom, with its balloon-like crinolines and its lovely Winterhalter ladies, is incomplete.

Of late years we have been given a Johann Strauss both on the boards ("Vienna Waltzes"), and on the screen. "The Bat", too, was played recently at Sadler's Wells, and an Opera Company gave "A Thousand and One Nights" at the Rudolf Steiner Hall.

Altogether it seems a pity that up to the present no little study of the Strausses should be available for the B.B.C. listener, who drops casually into a bookshop with the idea of running his eye over the shelves where the musical biographies are ranged, and asks for "something about Johann, not Richard".

It cannot be denied that the life of Johann Strauss, the son, as a man, was very fallible and human. He came of hot, unstable, mixed blood and in following a temperamental profession he was obliged to live an exotic if not downright neurotic existence. He was devoted to the sheer gilt and gingerbread of life throughout a hectic period of ups and downs in the effervescing society of nineteenth-century Vienna. Strauss was not a saint, nor a hero, and at times not altogether a gentleman. His morbid horror of death, and of the eternal problems or verities which the mere suggestion of it—such as the sight of a hospital or cemetery in the distance—might force upon the mind, was perhaps some indication of his own subconscious knowledge that the frivolous philosophy of a frivolous society translated into so many of his most bewitching melodies was ultimately worth nothing. Strauss was a man of iridescent froth, his veins filled with bubbling champagne.

But Johann Strauss the man, like Queen Anne, is dead, and need not be arraigned before the bar of human judgment, least of all the English section of it, which would be the last place where such a queer, gifted, spoiled, ill-regulated being would meet with the sort of insight which, knowing all, forgives all. The best of Strauss survives in his music, and it is just for the music's sake that the story behind it all has interest. Much of that music is extraordinarily lovely, and can hold its own, not only with the squeaks, blurtings, and hiccuping rhythms so popular at the present moment, but even with what is also quite beautiful in modern work. The present writer went into a little music shop the other day, in a small provincial town, to buy a work by Strauss exhibited in the window. It was the only piece there to which the sun and the dust had had nothing to say, and it looked clean and fresh, amid piles of the faded *ephemeridae* of the moment. "Lor' bless you," the salesman observed, "Strauss never lies long in the window, I can sell him every day."

Oddly enough, some of the Strauss music itself failed to reap full success when first produced, for the reason that it departed too widely from the accustomed and accepted. It struck out along new lines, burst old bonds, sought for newer and freer expression, and was, in fact, stigmatised as "futurist". For many years the most famous musical critic in Vienna, Dr. Hanslick, would have nothing to say to Strauss. He never missed an opportunity of decrying his work, and of prophesying its speedy extinction. It was only when the die-hard Hanslick, like the rest of musical Vienna, was forced at long, long last (largely through the apostleship of Strauss himself) to acknowledge the genius of Richard Wagner, that Hanslick made amends to the Kaiserstadt's own popular idol.

Strauss the musician survives. Of Strauss the man, one can only laughingly recall that when he died the Viennese (possibly somewhat apprehensive), unanimously threatened the Almighty with a boycott of Heaven if he were denied admittance!

. . . . .

Johann Strauss the younger was asked by a Publisher in Paris to write his own biography, but he declined. Strauss was not literary minded. He refused to read biographical eulogies published about himself at a time when Vienna was according him one jubilee after another. He had to put up with these heartfelt expressions of the public adoration, but he hated being lionised. He never cared to make the central figure in a drawing-room. No doubt he would have been modest in print.

. . . . .

The writer of the following pages may possibly be taken to task for not invariably translating German expressions, names of houses, titles of pieces of music. Where she has not done so it was for the reason that translation into any sort of idiom comparable to the original was impossible, so that to attempt it would have been pedantic and unnecessary, especially since it is not in the least imperative to understand a word to enjoy its flavour. A great deal of the Strauss flavour would be lost if titles like "Gunstwerber", and "Einheitsklänge" must necessarily be turned into English. The writer feels it does not matter in the least if they are not.

. . . . .

There must be plenty of people still living who retain some memory of Johann Strauss.

Only recently a lady stood without the railings of a great concert hall in Düsseldorf recalling an evening in summer but a few decades ago when, as a girl, she was taken thither to see and hear the Wizard from Vienna.

It was a grey rainy day when she told the story. Everything was wet and cheerless. The rain fell steadily on a sad-looking deserted public garden. A huge semi-circular auditorium in front of the ill-discerned façade of the distant "Halle" was filled with curving rows of upturned chairs. It was as dreary as only a pleasure resort can be out of the season, or in bad weather, or when its heyday has long gone by.

But the picture the visitor drew was of this place under a very different aspect, in July, sun-smitten, amidst charming verdure. It was crowded with a humming and expectant audience. Gay parasols, and the vast flower-bedecked hats that grandmothers to-day wore when they were twenty, filled those rows of chairs. All Düsseldorf had come to hear Johann Strauss.

The scene was one of the utmost sparkle and animation. The orchestra was assembled; the exciting interlude of tuning up was over . . . a tense moment of anticipation held the throng in thrall. . . .

Then suddenly he appeared, a lithe, dark figure, bowing double in response to a storm of welcome. It seemed the public could not sufficiently express its delight to have Johann Strauss actually there, ready to conduct his concert on the platform before them!

But at last even this acclaim subsided . . . now the Conductor was confronting his orchestra.

He raised his baton!

Then a gold wristlet flashed in the radiant sunshine. . . .

CHAPTER II

STRAUSS AND LANNER, 1804-'24

ONCE upon a time, getting on for a century and a half ago, there stood in a crooked alleyway of old Vienna an unpretentious inn or wine tavern named Zum Guten Hirt (The Good Shepherd).

It was in the Leopoldstadt, that bit of the city which sprawls lengthwise on the long narrow island between the Danube Canal and the main river, which once formed the old Ghetto. Zum Guten Hirt was a typical place of its kind. The alley, the Flossgasse, was paved, and that very badly, with a terrible sort of round little cobblestone called "Hüneraugenpflaster" (corns paving), and at night it was quite unlit. Very possibly Schubert and Beethoven had known of the Zum Guten Hirt and used it, for it could boast of good company. It was one of the innumerable Wirtshäuser whither the Viennese, rich or poor—here poor, high or low—here not too high, ever resorted for wine and song, friends, gaiety, shelter from the weather or from home. The entertainment was cheerful. Writers and composers frequented the Zum Guten Hirt, and music was always to be had there.

We may picture for ourselves a low-ceilinged little room, none too well lit, filled with tobacco smoke and the smell of a rough local wine called Vöslauer. It would be more or less filled with habitués, drinking and chatting, or scribbling on rather grubby scraps of paper, ruled for preference—but no matter—how and where they best could. In a corner a more or less disreputable looking fiddler

would be regaling the company with a rural dance tune
or two accompanied by someone with a clarinet or a guitar.

Music was always to be had in Vienna.

At this little inn it was of the more homely sort, consisting of those airs of the Austrian Alps, the Ländler, which
made their way down the long course of the Danube on the
river boats and barges. When the boats from Ulm conveying
passengers and livestock to Vienna crossed the frontier and
tied up at Linz, local Austrian musicians swarmed aboard,
and from thenceforth all the way down the river it was
their custom to regale the company with languorous melodies
played by a couple of fiddles, a guitar, a contrabass, and
possibly a clarinet. The banks were dotted by picturesquely
named little inns in every one of which the itinerant
"Musikanten" were as welcome as the guests they attracted
and entertained. Gradually the boats reached the outskirts
of Vienna only to encounter more and more of these genial
places of call.

Came Nussdorf, where the Canal branches from the river,
then the Stadt itself with all the Wirtshäuser of the crowded
streets and alleyways along the quays.

One of these was the Zum Guten Hirt.

It was run by an unassuming enough person called
Franz Strauss. Just five years after the Emperor Francis
II ascended the imposing throne of the Habsburgs this
insignificant subject of his married the daughter of a man
employed in the famous Imperial Riding School, a girl
named Barbara Tollmann.

Here in the Flossgasse their children were born, first a
girl named Ernestine, and then on the 14th of March,
1804, a boy whose baptismal name appeared in the local
parish register as Johann Baptist Strauss.

Things seem to have gone to pieces early with the Bierwirt,
for he threw himself into the river shortly after Johann was

born. The children were soon saddled with a stepfather, a man of the same calling, named Golder.

The boy grew up unhappily.

He soon evinced a strong inclination for music. It was but natural he should aim at becoming one of those cheery fiddlers who frequented the Flossgasse, but although the father and mother were not exactly anxious for him to take up work in their inn, under no circumstances at all, if they could help it, should "Schanerl" devote himself to this "verflixter Geigerei" (dratted fiddling), which led nowhere and often made a man a sot. Johann's longing for a fiddle was harshly repressed, and the boy presently found himself apprenticed to a bookbinder, Lichtschiedl by name, a good enough man in his way, but with a rough exterior and little patience for an unpromising youngster.

One charming German romance about this boy who was to become so famous ("*Des Walzerkönigs Liebestraum,*" by Rudolf Kleinecke) gives us a glimpse of him working in the bookbinder's shop, but working carelessly, unable or unwilling to take any interest in his trade, and getting into serious trouble with his master because he had misplaced some pages in a precious volume entrusted to Lichtschiedl to be rebound by the poet Grillparzer. The writer has it that the good wife here encouraged the boy's clandestine fiddling up in the attic when his master was out, and that she took his part stoutly against her exacting and exasperated man. However this may have been—and there is stuff enough for a dozen quite likely romances in the story of the Strausses, father and son—Lichtschiedl was no less concerned than his wife when Barbara Golder's Schanerl finally ran away.

Schanerl, or Schani, as they called the boy, ran away, but he did not run home. He was somehow fortunate enough to come across a man of some musical perception, who seems to have dropped in at the Zum Guten Hirt now and again—

according to the romance at least—and to have noticed the youngster and his passion for music in his mother's Weinstube.

This man, Polinschansky, rescued Schani from the streets and gave him music lessons.

Beyond this we know of no teaching received by one who was to become famous as "The elder Strauss". Johann's only real masters were his own genius, and life, and Vienna. It was by emulation alone, by practice, by imitation of the players he heard and saw all around him everywhere that the boy developed his gifts. He had little encouragement, and no prospects before him other than those of the river and the tavern player.

He had his ambitions, of course. At first their highest flight would be toward something better than the down-at-heel sort of thing which had caused his mother to set her face so doggedly against fiddling for him as a career. He must go farther than that for the sake of his own pride. He knew it in his bones that he could do a hundred times better given some sort of a start or chance. What he wanted to do was to get in somehow with one of the trios or quartettes, or even with one of the modest little orchestras whose name was legion, which lived by playing to the humbler folk all over the city wherever they foregathered to sit and enjoy themselves awhile. The Musikanten just got up at intervals and passed round a plate covered with a napkin. No one avoided it. The dance or the tune had been well worth paying for.

Neither winged nor weighted by too much teaching Johann became a resourceful and agile young violinist.

At the age of fifteen he joined the orchestra of a gentleman called Pamer who seems to have been much addicted to the flowing bowl. Pamer enjoyed a certain reputation, and Schani, who had hitherto only had a chance to play in public if a Church Choir had roped him in for an occasional Mass, felt himself in luck's way.

He was more in luck's way, indeed, than he knew!

In Pamer's orchestra he met a young fellow three years older than himself called Josef Lanner. But Lanner presently left Pamer and formed a trio with two cheerful individuals named Drahanek. They began playing on their own at an Inn called "Zum Grünen Jäger" (The green Huntsman), in the Leopoldstadt, and made such a reputation for themselves that the trio soon came into great request. Lanner was a composer. He had already allowed some of his peculiarly charming things to be given by Pamer's orchestra without troubling himself in the least for acknowledgements, but now his work began to have distinction and style, to take on a character of its own, and to attract attention. It attracted Schani. In Lanner he recognised a musician head and shoulders above the usual run of those he knew.

So young Strauss, too, left Pamer as soon as he found out that Lanner was willing to turn his "three-leaf" band into a "four-leaf" affair. With this step his career properly began.

For the next few years it was to be bound up intimately with that of a man far sweeter than himself in disposition, and very slightly inferior to himself in ability. Posterity will not forget Josef Lanner as long as it still cares to remember Johann Strauss the first.

Josef Lanner, the son of a glove-maker, was born in the St. Ulrich quarter of Vienna, not a mile from the Hofburg. House No. 6 in the Mechitaristengasse is pointed out as the place where he first saw the light.

By the time he accepted Schani Strauss as a colleague he had already more or less "arrived" in his profession, and offered exactly the type of success of which the boy had dreamed for himself in his most ambitious moments. The trio, now a quartette, was now playing in such resorts as

the "Wallischen Bierhause", near the Prater, and the "Reb-
huhn" in the Goldschmiedgasse, where the bosom friends
Schwind and Schubert delighted in Lanner's performances.
Josef was already somebody in Vienna.

He foretold great things for his new colleague, and the
two struck up another of those close musical friendships
with which the time seemed to abound. They took up their
abode together at a house called the Heumühle, and shared
in common not only their poor sticks and ragged scores and
aspiring souls, but also the famous single shirt which the
one could only sport when the other remained at home.
It was a cheerful gypsy existence in a laughter-loving city
where poverty was well accustomed to put on a smiling face.
The public soon found nicknames for the popular pair;
Lanner was "Flachskopf", the fair-haired one, and Strauss
"Morenschädel", the Blackamoor.

The spirit of Beethoven was in the air. Not far from
Lanner's birthplace the Master was living in the Trautsolin-
gasse. Lanner's first publisher was the very Diabelli who
commissioned the Thirty-three Variations. And his second
was Haslinger, a smallish individual with the sort of collar
called then-a-days a "Father murderer", who hated Diabelli
like the devil, and who lived in the Paternostergasse, where
pilgrims flocked to visit his great composer.

"These two men Lanner and Strauss," wrote Fritz Lange,
"in the beginning, just merely a pair of Wirtshausmusikanten,
who had to go round with the cap after their every piece;
two men who themselves sprang from the people, and who
had had little benefit of good musical education, were nevertheless inspired by that divine spark which soon burst
into flame and illumined everything far beyond their native
confines. . . ."

A study of the dance and folk music popular in Vienna
previous to their time reveals the fact that it lacked some of

the essential elements of rhythm. "For the men who concocted these tunes," continues Lange, "Weber's Invitation to the Dance had been written in vain, and Franz Schubert's delightful measures, which charm the whole world to-day, would have had but little appeal, to say nothing of the classical dance tunes of the musical giants." Strauss and Lanner began as suburban fiddlers giving their services outside the gates and fortifications. It was their ambition to conquer the Inner City, and they owed it to nothing but their own energy that they left the ranks of their colleagues still playing in the smoky taverns of the lower classes, and soared to the polite and fashionable sphere to which both later attained. They were the apostles of light-heartedness specially chosen to transplant the waltz from the inn (where, indeed, it was none too "polite" a dance), to the finest salons of select Viennese society. They "rooted out the weeds from the garden of popular melody with admirable thoroughness, and lavishly planted its wide paths with roses instead."

There has been some controversy as to the origin of the waltz, but there can be little doubt that it was Lanner who developed it as it now stands from the Ländler of the river boats, from the favourite folk measures of the time, such dances as the Langaus and the Deutschen, the Jewatsdorfer, and the Oberländler, and a dozen more whose quaint old names serve only to colour the Schani picture, and convey little to us now. Instead of a medley of eight-bar phrases in three-four time, Lanner adapted these so as to form a coherent whole, with an Introduction for concert purposes, and a Coda summing up the dance refrains.

Many years later Strauss the younger, writing about his father by way of Introduction to a collected edition of his works, gave a delightful account of Schani's and Lanner's methods of composition.

Strauss and Lanner Monument, Vienna.

"Musical composition at that time," he said, "was manifestly a simpler affair than at present. In order to produce a polka to-day one must make a study of the entire literature of music, not to say even of some philosophical system. Once upon a time it was only necessary for an idea to strike one, as the saying had it. And, oddly enough, something always did strike one. One had so much confidence in its doing so, that we older ones would often announce a new waltz for such and such an evening, of which on the morning of the appointed day not one note would yet have been written. In such a case the orchestra generally betook itself *en bloc* to the composer's lodging, and as soon as he had produced a theme and a few pages of the piece, every one would fall to practising and copying. Meantime the miracle of the inspiration repeated itself, and the second half was composed. Thereupon there would be a rehearsal of the whole, on the spot—the entire business only occupied a few hours—and as a rule it met with an enthusiastic reception upon production at night.

"Lanner hardly ever composed anything except after this fashion. When on occasion he fell ill, and unable to write, and was yet committed to a piece of work for which no single bar, only a few hours before, had as yet been written, he would just send my father the simple message, Strauss, what about an idea? The same evening the piece would be given—naturally as Lanner's—to be received with a fresh ovation."

It is amusing to reconstruct the scene of one of these impromptu rehearsals, at Strauss', when not at Lanner's, for they do not seem to have remained very long at the Heumühle.

Schani was probably living in some picturesque court or alley in a rabbit warren of a Hof, with low-ceilinged frowsty rooms, where the beds in the bachelor quarters never got

c

themselves made, and the windows everywhere were never opened, where the whole place reeked of goulasch, and of the general cheerful, noisy, undignified, lower-class Viennese human stew. It was a room into which Cruikshank might have introduced Mr. Swiveller had the muse of that essentially light-hearted gentleman ever directed his astonished steps in the wake of Josef's raiding orchestra.

Here they crowded in on each other's heels, introducing their instruments, the bigger ones—for the orchestra was always growing—as best they might; selected such vantage points as the circumstances, i.e. the bed and windowsill, might offer; and oblivious of cramped space and execrable light, started, as Strauss says, then and there to practise and transcribe. It was a tousled, shirt-sleeved orchestra, an orchestra very much behind the scenes, which fell to serious work until such time as Schani should fling down his flying scratching pen, thrust back his mop of raven hair, and grasping his bow, declare in the broadest of Viennese dialect that this was how the Coda should go. . . .

Strauss did quite a lot of work on the side. He was eager to make money; eager perhaps for independence. He gave music lessons, often fell in love, and out again, with his pupils; and he formed a quartette of his own which began to tout for engagements in the Leopoldstadt, and was taken on at the Zum Roten Igel. Lanner had no objection to offer to all this unless Strauss got too busy with his own affairs to put in time enough with the Lanner orchestra.

Lanner waxed in popularity day by day.

First he augmented his orchestra, then divided it into two, confiding the direction of the second to Strauss.

But dual management is always a risky affair. Strauss had already begun privately, like his friend, to write waltzes, and even if some of these may have been given as his own, many of them were ascribed to Lanner. The day however was over when this sort of thing did not matter. Johann was touchy and ambitious, and possessed the nerves of an artist. These misappropriations angered him. He became unwilling to go on with Lanner. . . .

The dance writers of the Vienna of that day, and the leaders of the innumerable and competitive little orchestras were a quarrelsome set. Moreover, there was no lack of partisanship on either side in the Lanner-Strauss case to foment the rivalry which unfortunately sprang up between them. Their public divided sharply into the "Lannerianer" and the "Straussianer".

Their association was wrecked.

They met for the last time at a resort called the Bock where lively rumours of the rift between them preceded their appearance. Some unfortunate trifle precipitated the unholy row which broke out upon the platform itself, the public looking on with the most intense interest. Fiddle bows were brandished, party cries resounded from all sides, and in a flash the thing resolved itself into a general mêlée in which musicians and host, guest and neighbour, vented their artistic wrath upon each other while the women urged on the combatants.

The outraged Lanner complained loudly, but thought better of the whole affair later on, and both sublimated his indignation and dissolved a six years partnership in a new waltz, the famous "Trennungs Walzer". Everything in Vienna wound up with a waltz.

From now on the two erstwhile friends went their separate ways. The Viennese public was passionately devoted to music enough to support any number of competitors for its favour.

Johann at twenty-one felt he had found his feet. He was longing to stand upon them, all the more because his latest love affair was turning out a trifle seriously, and he wanted to get married.

CHAPTER III

OLD VIENNA

IN order to set the story of the Strausses, father and son, against the background, political and picturesque of their time, it is necessary to take a look at Old Vienna. Vienna at the outset of the nineteenth century was still the quaint old Austrian city of the Napoleonic era. The famous Congress at which Metternich took care that every-one should dance rather than discuss, which broke up in the utmost consternation at the news of the Emperor's escape from Elba, was held when Schani Strauss was squirming under the rod of the bookbinder Lichtschiedl.

Only about the time of the death of this, the first Strauss, did that era of modernisation set in with which the joyous, fashionable and successful career of the younger Strauss was contemporary.

During the first half of the nineteenth century the Inner City remained encircled by the walls built in the thirteenth with the ransom money, so it is said, paid for Richard the Lionheart. As to art, it remained the old city of the classicists of German music, and as to politics, a place of arbitrary rule, full of violence and indolence and a good many vices. The districts beyond the outer fortifications, all overgrown to-day, were still rural in character, dotted with villages set among wine gardens. Beethoven wandering in the country could scare the cows with the vehemence of the inspiration driving him to frenzy, where now run streets and trams. Schubert, dumpy bespectacled little Schubert, could wander through cornfields catching throbbing ecstasies in the air to comfort him for one or another of his abortive love affairs, where to-day all is bricks or stucco and mortar.

But the Wienerwald remains, that lovely forest on the slopes of the last spurs of the Austrian alps; and the long slow course of the Danube beyond the city to the north still lies between it and the vast Hungarian plains of the far, far distance.

It was under Charles VI and Maria Theresa that Vienna developed throughout the eighteenth century into the political centre of the incredibly vast and heterogeneous Habsburg Empire. This Empress created the "Beamten-stadt", the city of imperial red tape and hide-bound officialdom, from which the whole, as from a huge office, was administered. The Hofburg was the office. Schönbrunn was the imperial residence. Maria Theresa's son Josef II, who followed her upon the throne, did much for Vienna, and attempted to do liberal things, as a Habsburg understood liberalism, for the people. Among other things he established German as the language to be spoken by all classes of society. Hitherto the aristocracy had used Latin, but since humanity only began at the baron, it scarcely mattered with what jargon people like the Bierwirt Strauss managed to get along.

But with the accession of this man's nephew—not the Bierwirt's but the Emperor's—the population, under 500,000 in number, again groaned under an absolutist government, and the ubiquitous spy system with which Metternich hoped to smother the least whisper of the French Revolution. It was Franz II who ruled in Austria during the first thirty-five years of the nineteenth century, a man not to be confounded with the Franz Josef who said, with dignity, on hearing of the murder of the Empress Elizabeth that God had spared him nothing! God spared him Kathé Schratt, (the Nazis have just deprived her of her last souvenirs), and Johann Strauss the younger. . . .

The Habsburg régime, founded not upon nationalism but upon loyalty to a dynasty, was upheld by the Church, the Army, and the Bureaucracy. It ruled by "despotism modified by laziness", as has been wittily said, and was characterised by procrastination, intrigue, guile and an utter want of principle. A dialect has coined a beautiful word for all this, the verb to "fortwursteln". It means to muddle along rather in a reprehensible sense than in a merely short-sighted one, but there is a laugh in it too.

There was no authentic source of news for the Viennese. War was a constant theme of discussion in the Wirtshäuser and the coffee houses. The common people were always being pressed into the armies. It was as unsafe, because of Metternich's agents, to talk in public of anything much save scandal, or the latest Italian or French comedy, as it may be to-day. History is forever repeating herself.

Prince Metternich, destined to dominate the affairs of Austria almost without control for thirty years, was Chancellor of State.

At this time the Inner City consisted of a few main streets in the neighbourhood of the Cathedral, St. Stefan, with its wonderful Gothic spire affectionately named "Old Stefferl", its shining roof of variegated tiles, and its great spread-eagle over the Choir. Then there was the vast conglomeration of the Hofburg with widespread flanking gardens. Everywhere the domes and spires of churches punctuated the huddled buildings. Scores of narrow lanes, ill-paved, ill-lit, ran between rows of houses whose dormer windows cut against the skyline. Tall baroque palaces, some of them very magnificent and laden with ornament, were flanked by disreputable tenements through whose cavernous doorways giving on to the granite setts of the pavé some of the interior frowstiness of rooms forever unaired gained upon the purity of the outer freshness.

There were few private or separate houses. All classes of the people lived in common in great blocks of buildings called Höfe, the poor at the top, the nobility on the best floors, and their servants in the rooms round the entrance halls. Vormärz Wien, i.e. the aristocratic part of Old Vienna, consisted of palatial houses jostled by the gabled houses of the richer burghers. There were vast religious establishments everywhere. It was during the eighteenth century that the architecture of Greater Vienna had taken on the brilliant character of the Baroque.

After the century-long menace of the Turks was overthrown—a menace against which the fortified city had served as an outpost of Christendom up to the middle of the eighteenth century—there was an outbreak of building activity here which still constitutes much of the glory of Vienna. The Turks had pushed up to the walls of the Inner City and laid waste all the suburbs without, so that this was the ground to be covered when that brilliant young Austrian architect Fischer von Erlach, fresh from five years study in Italy, set about creating a lovely Vienna for the Viennese. In fifty years he and his competitors and collaborators and followers had changed the face of things as they had been here, and left the city—the city into which Schani Strauss was born—much as we see it to-day, except for those new and modern suburbs forever pushing out farther and farther beyond the Leopoldstadt and the Prater over the river, and towards the Wienerwald on the other side.

It was the old Inner City with its wall, its gates, and bastions, and this Outer City of the Zopfzeit (Pigtail) period in architecture which Strauss senior and Lanner knew. The outer suburbs of to-day were then country districts. People got to places like Döbling and Grinzing, three or four miles out, in public vehicles called Zieselwagen which picked them up at a place called Am Hof in the Inner City and went jolting and bumping off to the villages. There were innumerable pleasure resorts all round Vienna where people went of a Sunday or holiday, or of an evening, to drink "Heuriger" (new wine on draught), or beer, to dance and sing and make love. Strauss the younger made his immortal début—as will be told in its place—at a famous café of this sort in Hietzing, called Dommayer's Casino, one very gay October evening in the year 1844.

It was during this period of rebuilding in the eighteenth century that Schönbrunn was created, together with that outstanding example of Baroque, the Imperial Library in the Hofburg, and many other palaces. Under Ferdinand I, however, who succeeded to the throne in 1835, there was no culture here other than music. Every book-lover was a potential criminal.

Under Metternich intellectuality was a dangerous occupation. Thus the only arts which could flourish in Vienna were those which might least lend themselves to political suspicion, music and architecture. This is not to say that music and architecture are not intellectual occupations. But that they flourished under the Habsburgs is another way of saying that neither the spy nor the policeman was exactly the right person to know how to deal with the spiritual content of a melody or a roll of stucco. Beethoven might write the ninth symphony with impunity, but no one dared write a book. Neither architecture nor music can be easily pilloried by the censor. The only music Strauss the elder ever wrote which got him temporarily into bad odour was the famous Radetzky March, because it meant something political. And the only music which hindered the younger Strauss' advancement was the gay revolutionary stuff he wrote in 1848—again because it meant something open to the crassest intelligence.

Neither Austria nor the eighteenth century could have produced Gothic art. It produced the Baroque, a very lovely style in its way however little it may appeal to the individual brought up on "The Bible of Amiens". Baroque has its own interpretation. But considered in the present connection it may be looked upon as a defiance, like the Habsburg Empire itself, of the laws of gravity; and again, like the Empire, as an amalgam of every material, stone, wood, stucco, guilding, paint, (without any necessary respect for the characteristics or limitations of any of them), pressed into the service of nothing more fundamental than ornament for ornament's sake.

Within the limits of such a city as this, then, flourished a "standing army of soldiers, a kneeling army of priests, a crawling army of spies", and a pleasure-loving irresponsible society. The people of Vienna had been rendered somewhat backboneless after years of ruthless elimination through religious persecution, of their stouter elements. They were subject, too, to the recurrence of the Föhn, a melting wind blowing down from the Alps calculated to enervate the most enterprising and energetic.

Here in Vormärz Wien the nobility of all Hungary, Bohemia, Galicia and Croatia possessed imposing residences, the windows of whose brilliantly-lit salons attracted crowds of the humbler citizens to stare and laugh and marvel night after night all through the winter season. Nothing could exceed the gaiety of these unending festivities and entertainments.

Just as society here in the preceding decades had revelled in Venetian drama, so the present generation doted on Italian music and opera, and everywhere Rossini, Bellini, and Donizetti held the Viennese stage. The Burg Theatre

was founded in 1776. Every spring some work was given
of the latest popular composer. The verdict of Vienna was
faultless and final. There used to be scenes of the wildest
enthusiasm in the Kärntnertor Theatre, which were by no
means to be attributed merely to the presence in the
audience of an enormous number of Italians at that time
resident in the city.

The other extreme to this exotic type of life was shown,
as Wagner shrewdly observed, by the wholesome and
native enjoyment exhibited in the suburban theatres in
response to the fantasias of Raimund and the satires of
Nestroy, accompanied as these were by native Austrian
music. One had to leave Vormärz Wien behind and betake
oneself to the less pretentious regions of the city where the
less important people lived, or those of no importance at
all—like the Gastwirt Strauss, or Golder and his wife and
children—to witness exactly the same scenes of gaiety and
enjoyment on a somewhat more modest scale.

The love of the Viennese for music had long made the
Austrian capital a mecca for musicians. It had attracted
Glück, Hayden, Mozart, Beethoven and very many others.
There was employment for such men with wealthy patrons
of all sorts. Many of the princely establishments in Vienna
maintained their own orchestras, or private Chapel choirs
or dance bands, or the quartettes and trios which dispensed
music in the dining-room. There was a great deal of music-
teaching to be done. The early life of the gifted boy born
to the Bierwirt in the Flossgasse synchronised with the
lives of many an ornament to Viennese artistic society in the
eighteen twenties—with that of the poet Grillparzer, of Vogl
the singer, of Spawn and Schober, of the charming Frölich
sisters and the members of the Schubert circle in general.

In spite of all this, there was, as we have seen, little of
general culture in Vienna at the beginning of the nineteenth

century. The material prosperity of the Empire was much retarded by the political confusion which followed Napoleon's overthrow.

The Congress of Vienna was just as remarkable for the brilliant society "season" which attended it, as for its assemblage of crowned heads and European diplomats. Miss Lilian Harvey and her bewitching song "Love, Life, and Laughter", from the film "Congress Dances", may well serve us, in this connection, for the very impersonation of that gay world which the young Strauss later determined to conquer.

No one would gather a correct idea of Vienna at the opening of the nineteenth century from any such picture as that drawn by the Comte de la Garde Chambonas, in his spirited account of this great occasion and of all the notabilities it attracted. That light-hearted observer was so caught up in the "irresistible whirl of uninterrupted pleasure" which signalised the Congress that he seems to have seen nothing of the realities of things behind that hectic gaiety, freedom from care, and happiness which appeared to be the normal condition of Viennese society.

"In September, 1814," he informs us, "Vienna assumed an aspect which was as bright as it was animated. Numberless magnificent carriages traversed the city in all directions, and, in consequence of the restricted size of the capital, constantly reappeared. Most of them were preceded by those agile forerunners, in their brilliant liveries, who are no longer to be seen anywhere except here, and who, swinging their large silver-knobbed canes, seemed to fly in front of the horses. The promenades and squares teemed with soldiers of all grades, dressed in the varied uniforms of all the European armies. Added to these were the swarms of the servants of the aristocracy in their gorgeous liveries, and the people crowding at all points of vantage to catch a momentary glimpse of the military and diplomatic celebrities constantly passing in and out of the frame of the variegated picture. Then, when night came, the theatres, the cafés, the public resorts were filled with animated crowds, apparently bent on pleasure only, while sumptuous carriages rolled hither and thither, lighted up by torches borne by footmen perched behind, or still preceded by runners who had, however, exchanged their canes for flambeaux. In almost every big thoroughfare there was the sound of musical instruments discoursing joyous tunes. Noise and bustle everywhere."

All this would make a good screen scene in contrast, say, to an interior at the Zum Guten Hirt. But the Comte himself supplies the contrast, which also does something to round off the picture of Vienna at this period. He tells us that every available hotel and private lodging was besieged. Prices rose exorbitantly. Thanks to his being received in the "magnificent residence" of an English friend the Comte found "all the comfort which the former had transported thither from his own country, both the language and the condition of things it represented, being very little known throughout the rest of Europe." The back scene of all this magnificence even at the Hofburg and at Schönbrunn was probably squalid enough.

"Foreigners," the Comte recorded, "are generally well treated in Vienna. The inhabitants are cordially hospit-able—— In return for this strangers are only asked to refrain from speaking or acting against the Government—woe to him who transgresses those laws of prudence . . .! Fortunately the Austrian Government found a powerful auxiliary in this general pursuit of pleasure. In reality little or no attention was paid to diplomatic discussions," either during the Congress, or at any other time.

Of the Prater the Comte wrote: "It abutts on the fau-
bourgs of Vienna, and is situated on one of the islands of
the Danube which virtually constitutes its boundary.
It is throughout planted with century-old trees affording
a majestic shade and keeping the huge greensward from
being scorched by the sun. It is crossed in every direction
by imposing avenues. As at Schönbrunn, and at the majority
of like resorts in Germany, herds of deer browse peacefully.
. . . To the left of the Prater, on entering it from the city,
there is an immense lawn set apart for the display of fire-
works, and to the right there is a circus capable of accom-
modating several thousands of spectators. Facing one
is a large avenue of chestnuts bordered on each side by
elegant buildings, including a number of shops, cafés, and
casinos where the Viennese can indulge to their hearts'
content in their well-known love of music."

To round out this sketch of the pre-Franz Josef Vienna,
the darker aspect of things must not be ignored.

Vienna was full of gay places of ill repute. The finest of
these, the two most famous ballrooms, the Apollosaal and
the Sperl, are both closely bound up with the Strauss story.
A description of them, together with one of the beautiful
Redoutensaal, the ballroom at the Hofburg, whither both
Strausses finally attained, can be left until the first Johann's
ambition has carried him as far as their gilded and equivocal
portals.

The streets of Vienna had a bad reputation until the
introduction of gas lighting in 1843, (the year in which Lanner
died), did something to mitigate the scandal.

The morals of Vienna left much to be desired, but that is a
pointless remark since it might be made about any great city
at any period. What does occasionally cross the mind of
the student of the Strauss era is the question as to whether
there could be said to be any serious religious life in Vienna

at that time. The city abounded with religious houses, but
what part, if any, did religion play in the lives of men like
Strauss and Lanner, and in those of their devotees? They
were all nominally Catholics, of course. . . .

It so happened that a very humble sort of man had been
leading a life of goodness and of apostolic zeal for men's
souls in Vienna just before this time. The Strauss public
had been to some extent also the public of the sainted
Priest Clement Maria Hofbauer. One successful operatic
librettist had actually "got religion", and turned priest,
and taken to preaching in the Viennese pulpits with Knox-
like severity against the frivolities of the time. But no echo
of all this resounds however faintly in the Strauss story.
So we need not pursue it here.

CHAPTER IV

THE ELDER STRAUSS, '25-'37

JOHANN STRAUSS married a girl three years younger than himself in July, 1825. He had met her when playing in Lanner's orchestra in her father's inn.

This was Anna Streim, the daughter of a man who rose from the position of a coachman to be the proprietor of a well-known resort Zum Roten Hahn (The Red Cock) in Liechtenthal, a suburb of Vienna. It was through his mother that Johann Strauss the younger derived much of his genius. Like many of the musicians of one of the most polygot cities on earth, Strauss was only half Viennese.

The story of the grandmother Anna Maria Streim, is sufficiently wild and romantic. She was born in Madrid, and was said to have been the daughter of a Spanish nobleman who killed a still bigger Grandee than himself in a duel somewhere in the seventeen-sixties and was obliged with his wife and family to fly the country and adopt a plebeian name. He found a position in Vienna as cook in the household of Duke Albert von Teschen. The sons and daughters of this so-called "Rober" married in due course, but into even more humble circumstances. It is quite possible that this legendary Hidalgo was no more than a wandering gypsy after all, and that cooks and coachmen were really his social superiors. The guitar with which Anna Streim used to sing and play was long preserved in the Strauss family. Whatever the truth may be about the origin of Johann's mother, the fact of his having dark blood in his veins was quite sufficiently attested by his swarthiness

47

and the peculiar witchery of his "charming malicious glance". All the children of the first Johann and Anna had in them this strain of Moorish darkness to say nothing of the remote sources of their musical inspiration.

Immediately upon severing his connection with Lanner, and upon his marriage, Johann Strauss gave up playing in public for a while, and became a music-teacher. He is so described in his son's baptismal register. He taught both the violin and the piano. Later on these lessons of his, published by Haslinger (the Viennese Ricordi), became well known, went through many editions, and attained a good sale.

He had by no means, however, given up his cherished plan of being the leader of his own dance band. Only a few months later, in Fasching (Carnival time), 1826, we find him conducting an orchestra of fourteen men, which at once began the conquest of Vienna. It was soon in universal request, and the young man's every evening was fully booked up.

His first work, the "Tauberl Walzer", was played in a garden restaurant called "Zu Zwei Tauben" (The Two Doves), in the summer of that year, and it met with immediate success. It was quickly followed up by a series of equally delightful compositions, each one of which was rapturously received by the public. With the famous "Kettenbrücken Walzer" (named after the Guesthouse at Kettenbrück), Johann Strauss won for himself a place in the first rank of his colleagues or rivals. "That means a good deal," says Lange, for although much of the contemporary dance music was not of the best order or in the best taste, "perhaps the old bastion-girdled Kaiserstadt never possessed so many men all writing waltzes together at any previous time."

At the age of twenty-five young Strauss stood at the head of his profession and had conquered fashionable and select

Vienna. He transferred himself from the dance "Lokalen" of the suburbs and the outer city to the smartest resort of contemporary gay society, when the proprietor of "Sperls" concluded a contract with him for six years. This well-known and well-patronised resort of fashionable Vienna had not a good reputation, but it meant the zenith of his ambition to a young man who was already the father of three children, Johann, Josef and Nelli.

The first—the famous Johann the Younger—was born not two miles from St. Stefan in a modest little two-storied house in the suburb of St. Ulrich, No. 15 Lerchenfelder Strasse, otherwise called Zur Goldenen Eule (The Golden Owl).

The young married pair had gone through a good deal in the way of parental opposition on her people's part and Johann was working desperately hard to justify his daring in having captured the heart of the daughter of a man who thought a good deal of himself as the proprietor of the well-known Zum Roten Hahn and nothing at all of Johann.

A quaint old picture gives us an idea of the "Eulenhaus" in which Johann the Second first saw the light. Sandwiched in between somewhat more pretentious neighbours, it yet presented a considerable façade to the street upon which it directly abutted. Long rows of shuttered and uniform windows, and a pentroof with three small dormers, lighted the various apartments of this human warren in old Vienna. It is not to be supposed that the struggling young musiker, Strauss, occupied the best of these. Anna lay in a fusty enough room, none too clean, none too airy, none too quiet, and it was by the Austrian Mrs. Gamp of the period that his squealing red-faced heir—heir in genius and fame if nothing else—was presented to the anxious father.

D

Very possibly something learned has been written by somebody on the philoprogenitiveness or the reverse of artists. These are men and women to whom the children of their brains count more than those of the body. The writer, the painter, the musician, especially when poor, unknown, inspired and struggling, has not much use for an incidental and inevitable family. But nevertheless the family appears, to encumber his feet and exasperate his nerves.

So it fell out with this pair, Anna and Johann Strauss. Their firstborn was speedily followed by the rest of the family. Johann had little time for dalliance over the baby, although the mother seems to have been imbued from the beginning with a special pride in her "Schanerl". This developed later into that strong support and understanding without which there might have been no successor to the first Waltz King.

Josef Strauss, one of Johann's famous brothers, and in many ways the gentlest and most humanly engaging member of a temperamental family, was born on August 20th, 1827, in a house called Zum Ritter (The Knight). After that the parents moved to the Leopoldstadt, and we hear of them first in the house Zum Weissen Wolf (The White Wolf), then in the Einhorn (The Unicorn), on the Karmeliterplatz where a little girl, Theresa, saw the light.

The Apollosaal was in the Leopoldstadt.

In the time of the old Emperor Franz—not the Franz Josef of the second half of the nineteenth century—the Apollosaal was the most important ballroom in Vienna. Its hey-day lasted from about 1808 to 1834 when it gave place to the Sperl, and was turned into a soap factory.

To gain some idea of what a fashionable resort of this kind meant about the time that the elder Strauss emerged into the full limelight of Viennese society, and, indeed, took upon himself to give it an entirely new cachet, a few words of description must suffice.

The Apollosaal, says Decsey, "comprised five enormous ballrooms, forty-four large drawing-rooms, three colossal conservatories, and thirteen kitchens. Marvellous greenery and flowers abounded everywhere amid waterfalls and grottoes, and a lake with real swans upon it. Garlands, flowering shrubs, and again more flowers turned the place even in winter (and Viennese winter!) into a veritable garden, the whole being reminiscent of nothing so much as the luxury of ancient Rome. These huge salons of the Apollosaal displayed innumerable chandeliers of brilliant lustres. Triumphal arches on marble pillars led from floor to floor, the names of the Emperor and Empress were emblazoned everywhere together with the heraldic insignia of the city." Of the Sperl which carried on another thirty years after the fading of the Apollosaal a witty observer once remarked: "Here the bones of our forefathers do not rest—but danced."

If the whole life of the Viennese must be described as a holiday, what is to be said of the Carnival, especially when every good citizen had it impressed upon him as a "Christian duty" to distinguish "Fasching" from the drab monotony of the rest of the year. The Fasching festivities were concluded under many heads, such as public balls, masquerades, private balls, smaller private dances and "conversation" dances.

Here, indeed, was scope for the peculiar Strauss talent —here it found a sphere only one degree less inspiring than that of the Imperial Court itself. During one Carnival alone, over seven hundred and seventy-two balls were given, attended by 200,000 people, about half the entire population of the city. Vienna abounded with resorts very much like Vauxhall in London, where dancing and refreshment were enjoyed partly under cover, partly in the open air.

Once Director of the Dance Music at Sperl's, Johann was in a position to introduce all sorts of innovations. The new waltzes demanded a new type of elegance altogether. This ambitious young man with his black cube-like head, pale drawn cheeks, dark eyes, and immaculate linen was no shabby "Musiker" like so many who had preceded him. No one frequenting the dance floors at Sperl's could have got himself up beforehand at the hands of his barber and tailor with more punctilious care than the conductor of the orchestra.

The result was amazing.

Every affair at Sperl's was crowded out. . . . The "Strauss-Zauber" (Strauss craze) began.

In the autumn of the year 1830 the young Polish pianist Chopin came to Vienna with the intention of giving a series of concerts. But he wrote disgustedly to his parents that the Viennese had no time for serious music, Lanner and Strauss had captivated the entire public with "nothing but their waltzes".

Then, two years later, came Richard Wagner, aged nineteen. He "fell" for Strauss at once, and never forgot the impression made upon him by the dapper Direktor at the Sperl. Vienna he considered "the home of an original and indigenous productivity". Everywhere there was an ecstasy of magical new melody in the air. "The Waltz," he found, "is a more powerful narcotic than alcohol. The very first bars set the whole audience aflame. The thing passes belief. And this amazing Strauss himself, this bewitching fiddler, this spirit incarnate of Viennese popular music, trembles from head to foot, like Pythia on the tripod, at the opening of the piece. The warm summer air in Vienna was full, for me, of little else but Strauss and Zampa."

This was the source, perhaps, of some part of the Wagnerian inspiration itself.

Strauss was overwhelmed with work. At Carnival time he often directed three orchestras, rushing from one to the other, or entrusting this, that or the other—under his own eye—to a chosen lieutenant. He had an orchestra himself of a hundred musicians, out of which he chose a corps d'élite which he wrought to a pitch of perfection never yet known in Vienna, where dozens of well-known conductors, men like Fahrbach, Morelly, Bendel and Ballin, each with an enthusiastic public following of his own, already occupied the field.

When it is realised that the whole fame and pride of a Viennese dance orchestra depended upon the variety and freshness of its repertory, and that its reputation sank at once should a single piece be too frequently repeated, it can be imagined what a demand this made upon the versatility of the Direktor.[1]

"Father Strauss," Decsey tells us, "lived apart from the family in a little room of his own." His affairs demanded it. After a hectic evening in the ballroom, "he would sit about late into the night with friends. He did not lend himself to Pantagruellian revels, but no musician went to bed before his nerves were all in rags. He would sleep of a morning. Then came visits and callers. Next he must write —every big ball demanded something new—worried and driven. Strauss had no time or interest for his family. Often he knew nothing of what was going on at home. Irritable and contrary, he flared into temper for the slightest thing, cursed the musical life, and only heard at second hand what sort of geniuses his boys promised to be".

[1] Between them Strauss and Lanner had driven the old "Cholera Kapelle" (Stomach ache bands) of the suburbs right out of the field. It is interesting to note that even at the height of his success Strauss continued to do his best to make up for the paucity of his musical education. He went in for a serious course of technical instruction under the famous master von Seyfried; reaped much profit from it, and prosecuted his study of the violin under Professor Jansa.

At the age of twenty-seven Vienna had grown too small for him. His fame spread far and wide and he was pressingly invited to accept engagements abroad. He betook himself and his orchestra to Pesth, Dresden, Leipzig, Berlin, and made a tour in Southern Germany. In Leipzig an unknown admirer came up to him after the concert and begged to see the score. It was Mendelssohn.

. . . . .

Meanwhile little Johann at home was growing up. His mother was accustomed to take the children in summer to stay with their grandmother at Salmannsdorf not far from Vienna, all among the mountains and the forests where a pleasant ivy-grown house served the family as a country retreat. Here Johann, at six, picked out a little waltz tune for himself on an old "Tafelklavier", which his mother wrote down. They called it "Erster Gedanke" (First Thought). This little piece was given "on the air" some time ago (how astonished Frau Anna would have been), in the course of a Radio résumé of Johann's life and work.

Between 1825 and 1835 five children were born to Johann and Anna Strauss. One of them, Ferdinand, died when only two years old. The three boys, Johann, or "Schani" as they came to call him, Josef, and Edouard (born March 15th, 1835), were all singularly musically gifted. As quite little things they betook themselves to the piano, and learnt to scribble minims and crotchets far more readily than their ABC.

We get a picture of their home in the house (No. 17 Taborstrasse) at the sign of the Golden Stag, the Hirschenhaus, where they lived from '34 to '86. This was one of the immense communal houses of Vienna. Four stories high with dormers in the roof and two street frontages in long perspectives, it comprised seventy-seven flats built round a courtyard where barrel organs played incessantly and the children swarmed.

At the corner of the two streets the building stood out in a large round bow from the basement to the eaves. The ground floor was given up to shops and cafés. On the second floor the windows—casements, of course, opening outwards—were round-headed and separated from the long line of those above with their small triangular pediments, by a bold line of demarcation in the masonry. The top floor windows under the handsome eaves were perfectly plain.

Here the Strauss family was to remain for many years, and to weather many vicissitudes.

Parts of the Leopoldstadt were situated on low-lying ground, subject to inundation when the ice in the river broke up in the spring, and the Danube and its Canal just above Nussdorf became flooded from the snows melting on the mountains and swelling the contributary streams. At times like these the townsfolk had to make use of improvised stages and plank bridges to get about, or they were even forced to take to the "Zillen" and "Schinakeln", the canoes and lighter craft of the river. If the floods were very severe the military would be called out to aid the waterside men, and to fling pontoons over the flooded streets. The people in the houses would be marooned.

In the "Liebestraum" we hear of Strauss having no mind, one night, to pick his way home in the early hours of a dark winter's morning over the precarious boards of the Leopoldstadt alleys. This was before the family was decently housed at the Sign of the Golden Stag, before the struggling young Bandmaster had picked up any plums in the way of really good engagements. He decided to pass the night in the Inner City at the lodging of one of the members of his orchestra. Waking late next day, undisturbed

for once by the children, he went out to a near-by eating-
house for a much-needed snack before once more screwing
himself up to face the noise and discomforts of home. The
Strausses were uncomfortably cramped in quarters none
too safe from the river, and the nervous, irritable, over-
worked young father was often tempted to regret the old
comparatively care-free days when he and Lanner and their
companions could make a dance and a song of whatever
might befall.

Johann and Lanner had long got over their historic
"Krach" at the Bock[1]. They had often met since, of course,
and they frequently paid each other the compliment of
playing each other's pieces. But to-day Strauss was off
colour. He sat down grumbling to his companion over their
belated breakfast that his mother had not been so far out,
years ago, about this "verflixter Geigerei". Music was all
very well pursued for pleasure, or to sit and listen to, but
it was the very devil to have to make a living by. He
would take good care to knock any such notion out of his
own boys' heads, particularly out of that young monkey
Schani's! Talking, with some recovery of spirits, of Lanner,
Strauss' first violin remarked that the Meister's old chief
happened at the moment to be only a stone's throw away,
at the Silver Café, together with Castelli (an actor con-
vulsing all Vienna just then at one of the theatres), and
Deinhardstein, and Raimund. . . . Where-upon Strauss
promptly settled his reckoning where they were, and betook
himself to this charmed and congenial circle.

It had such an effect upon his volatile spirits, that the
resulting causerie spun itself out all the afternoon. They
sat over the coffee together, that group, hour after hour,
until Lanner suddenly discovered he must bolt or he would

[1] They made up their quarrel on the occasion of Lanner's marriage to
Franziska Jahns on Nov. 24th, 1828. Lanner's marriage turned out very
much like Johann's.

be late for an engagement, and the same shock struck Strauss.

The waters were out in the Leopoldstadt. Frau Anna had been relying on Johann last night to bring provisions home after the concert. But the circumstance had gone out of his head and now the matter must wait again. . . .

When Johann finally reached home, thirty-six hours late, it was to find his own apartment crowded out with the folk from downstairs whom the waters had forced to take refuge with his wife. So the provisions, if ever they got there, if he managed to remember them at all, must have come in particularly handy.

Strauss had, indeed, already arrived at the stage of finding married life a drag upon him, and a disappointment. His nerves were in rags as soon as he got home. He worked too hard, his genius was cruelly exploited, he never had any peace. Noise, worry and excitement were making a wreck of husband and father.

The atmosphere in the Strauss flat was usually thundery. Johann was irritable and despotic, and although Edouard, the youngest son, in a volume of reminiscences made a valiant effort in later years to dispel the legend of fear and unhappiness reigning there, it cannot be disputed that the younger Johann's obstinate pursuit of music was the cause of many a scene and quarrel.

Although the father allowed both Johann and Josef to receive piano lessons, he laid no stress on them, and was much more anxious about their general education. He even took a certain amount of pride in the boys' duet playing—when the music publisher Haslinger admiringly drew his attention to it. On one occasion, when little Johann helped him out with the resolution of an unsatisfactory passage in a waltz, laying his hand on the keys and asking, "How about this, Father—won't that go?" he laughed, accepted, and exclaimed, "What a monkey! I'd better do your lessons, and you can write my waltzes for me!"

Nevertheless Strauss set his face resolutely against Johann thinking of music as a career. In a city of so much musical competition, where Schubert had starved for years, he was convinced that no one's bread tasted so bitter, nor was moistened with so many tears of disappointment as that of the composer. Every leaf in his laurel wreath was plucked from a thorn bush. Let but two failures occur, but two dances fall short, and the writer was done. Strauss knew his Vienna.

He meant his son to be spared this if he could. He set before him, instead, the ideal of the bourgeois Austrian—some official post with a pension. He wanted Johann to stand on a solid basis in life, and to have the commercial education which would fit him for a position in a bank. As a matter of fact Strauss had made social contacts which would have assured a good opening of this sort for his eldest-born.

Johann first went to school at the "Trivialschule" but at eleven he was sent to the "Schottengymnasium", where from '36 to '40 he did fairly well, and was quite a good boy.

Meanwhile, however, all sorts of secret musical happenings were going on at home, aided and abetted by a mother whose instinct about the boy led her to make no mistake. Anna Strauss, "a pretty Viennese with vivacious dark eyes and her hair done in the queer Chinese style of the eighteen-twenties, might not have been an absolutely pattern house-wife for ever cooking and cleaning, but for all that she was a manager. She was not going to limp through life"; she was quite capable of seeing things with her own eyes. She was, at that day, a modern, and it was to her that Johann owed his own passionate appreciation of Wagner. Anna Strauss took the boy's part in the strife which arose between him and his father.

By courtesy of the Director of the Historical Collections of the City of Vienna.

CARICATURE OF JOHANN STRAUSS, VATER.

"The boy," says Decsey, "must have had fishes' blood in his veins, rather than that of a born musician, not to have been intrigued by the entire array of orchestral instruments even to the double bass and the drums, which stood in his parents' bedroom. Here he saw his father perpetually busied about them, heard nothing but the 'shop' talked by the endless stream of his father's visitors, and conceived no vision of a greater splendour than one day to be like them, one day to outdo this wonderful father at his own game!"

Secretly he got hold of a violin—no one could write dance music unless he could fiddle—and cast about him for means of earning a little money. For a few Kronen he taught a tailor's son and the daughter of a neighbour in the Hirschenhaus flats to play the piano, and was thus able to pay his own father's first violin, a man called Amon, for lessons in his turn. The thing had to be kept deadly dark, or Amon would have been summarily kicked out of the orchestra.

It was Amon who made young Johann a dandy. He laid stress on the violinist's appearance and deportment, and exacted practice before the looking-glass. All this had become the rage at the moment. One day, however, as the boy planted before the glass was bowing with the utmost elegance at his command the door was wrenched open and his infuriated father burst in.

"What's all this fiddling I hear? You *will*, will you?" he shouted, and wrenched the instrument out of the boy's hand.

A fearful but not uncommon row followed, and for the time being the father appeared to get the best of it.

At sixteen Johann was sent to a technical school where his nose was to be kept to the grindstone of commercial arithmetic, book-keeping and business correspondence.

He only allowed himself to be thus "commercially mis-handled" for two abortive years, to please his father, since his mother privately consoled him by the gift of another violin—and that one belonging to her husband himself! So the secret practising went on, and the cleft in the family between man and wife, son and father, grew ever wider and wider.

The only part of his school work which appealed to the youngster was the singing-class. He got into trouble one day either for scribbling refrains in his exercise book, or for some boyish piece of impudence, and was sent off with the injunction not to show his face at school again.

To Schani this spelt release and freedom. The hour he had longed for struck at last!

He was unable to profit by it, however. The elder Strauss was still bent on fighting a sort of rearguard action. Johann, in disgrace, was condemned to private tutoring at home. . . .

Johann the elder lived, now, more and more only for the ball-and-concert-room. He had no use for a quarrelsome home overfull of lively youngsters. The make of man he was, the times, and the feverish career he pursued to such heights of giddy success led almost inevitably to domestic tragedy. That sooner or later he should leave his wife— the mother who sided with her son against him—is easily to be understood, but that the idol of Viennese society should leave her for a common little modiste out of the slums presents quite a problem even in temperamental and artistic psychology. Yet this is, indeed, what happened.

There is no doubt there was a great deal of unhappiness in the Strauss home. Johann was temperamental, irritable, volatile, a man whose very profession made of him a joy for the whole world outside, and a terror for the small one within. Money worry had a great deal to do with it. What-ever he earned as the bandmaster most in demand in Vienna

was not so considerable that Strauss's overhead expenses
could easily be met. He had his orchestra to pay, and his
copyists, as well as the family to support. His chief
customers, the proprietors of cafés and dancing-rooms,
and society hostesses, paid him as little as they could
decently or indecently manage, and his publishers exploited
him shamelessly.

The scenes that took place at home did little to help a
worried composer. His inspiration was checked and his
fantasy destroyed. "A waltz king needs sunshine," said
his friend Herr Karl Friedrich Eusebius Hirsch, who often
dropped in on the Strausses and did what he could to allay
the misery poor Frau Anna suffered from gossip. Every
day tales, true or untrue, were brought to her ears, of her
husband's flirtations—to say the least of them. The women
of Vienna were at his feet, especially the young and pretty
ones, and when sometimes in despair Johann would let the
quill drop from his feverish fingers, abandon some in-
tractable resolution or finale, furiously slam the door of
the flat behind him, and betake himself to the town, it
was only to run the danger by daytime that it was at once
his fate and his business to run at night.

It would be easy to imagine a dozen frivolous occasions
when the exasperated husband and father first exchanged
a stimulating glance with some pretty little modiste of the
Viennese suburbs, which instantly consoled him for his
domestic worries, and banished them from his mind. We
know how inflammable those Viennese musicians used to
be—how "Franzerl" Schubert's heart would go up in
flame at a glance. It might have been in the Prater on a
Sunday afternoon, or round any bandstand of his own
where music, laughter, and light-hearted love-making were
all in the order of the day. Johann was the universal idol.
Neither history, nor what is more important here, gossip,

records when and where he first encountered Emilie Trampusch, a bewitching little orphan who was presently led to
confide to him that she lived with an old ogre of an uncle.
At first she hesitated to reveal that she was only a milliner,
for the marvellous Herr Kapellmeister whose breath-
taking attention she had managed to attract might have
been rebuffed by such an admission. We can picture her
looking very much like a Cruikshank drawing of a pretty
girl, say Kate Nickleby, in an early edition of Dickens,
in poke bonnet and curls, with a shawl drawn over shapely
shoulders, ridiculous little laced shoes and a crinoline, like
the three lovely maidens in "Lilac Time" who frolicked with
Grillparzer, Schwind, Vogl, and the modest Schubert, in that
charming play.

An intriguing encounter, somewhere, led to something
more than a gingerbread plot for a Viennese operetta.
A liaison sprang from it which was to become a lasting
entanglement. Johann was positively attracted by the girl,
and very soon the worst rumours which could reach poor
Frau Anna's ears were justified. A secret understanding
was reached between these two. For some time Strauss
left Emilie among her own surroundings, then he trans-
planted her to a little flat in the Kumpfgasse, just across
the canal and the Schwedenbrücke, without definitely
abandoning his own home in the Hirschenhaus. But
Emilie, it seems, grew restless, longing to see something
of the gay life to which her protector belonged. He only
managed to hold open scandal at bay—for a time—by
humouring her and taking her with him, that is to say,
by allowing her to precede him, upon an occasional visit
to Hamburg or Berlin.

Herr Eusebius Hirsch, that long standing friend of
Johann's, who soon earned for himself the affectionate
nickname of "old Lampenhirschl", and who did his best as

long as he could to act as go-between when the rift in the
Hirschenhaus began, and slowly widened, was an official
in the service of the Imperial Library. Like everybody else
in Vienna he had had his own dreams of a musical career,
and as a young fellow of seventeen had received lessons
in harmony from Beethoven. The course had soon been
given up through want of cash, probably, on the pupil's
part, or want of patience on that of the Master. Later
there came along a brilliant young Musiker only too ready
to do Hirsch the good service of knocking some of his
attempts at composition into shape—and remarkably
pleasant shape too—in return for a few Kronen. A friendship sprang up between the two which was to prove of much
assistance to the harassed and driven father of a growing
young family.

Strauss could never make money enough to satisfy Frau
Anna as well as to meet the expenses of his profession.
To pay his musicians and his copyists came first; after
that the family had to take its sketchy chance. The money
might have sufficed, carefully and properly husbanded
and laid out, but now there was Emily Trampusch, and
finances were never the artist's strong point. Strauss
muddled them from first to last. Hirsch, however, did
what he could to act for Strauss as manager and publicity
agent. He conceived the same idea which had formed an
added attraction to the early Offenbach concerts in Paris,
and arranged for gas illuminations at Strauss' evening
entertainments. Hence his nickname.

CHAPTER V

THROUGHOUT this period the Strauss craze was ever growing. There were whole weeks together —doubtless much enjoyed and utilised at home —when the Viennese dance king was abroad with his orchestra, and all they heard of him in the Hirschenhaus were the rumours of ever greater and greater successes. On the intermittent occasions of his return to Vienna, the boys, Johann and "Pepperl" (Josef), either had to lay their own darling pursuits entirely aside and pretend a dutiful absorption in study, or domestic strife flared up afresh.

Although at the very height of his popularity, and worked almost to death, so numerous were his engagements, and so ubiquitous was the demand for him, Strauss was always at his wits' end for money. He paid his orchestra well: when on tour he travelled with them *en Prince*. But he had no head for finance, and without the good offices of his friend Hirsch, it is to be doubted if he would have managed to spare even the little he did for the maintenance of his two homes. Strauss delighted the whole world but sorely disappointed the two women who looked to him to support them and his children. It was with the bold idea of gambling on his own genius and his own inspiration that he conceived the unheard-of plan of leaving Vienna for a long time, of leaving Germany, indeed, and seeking both recognition and monetary success in Paris and London. This was, for that period, a tremendous undertaking, one fraught with all the delays and hardships and inconveniences of travelling by stage coach often in savage weather.

Strauss left Vienna in the autumn of '37 with twenty-six companions. The city gave him a great send-off, and then settled down to wait for the news of astounding triumphs in Paris where their idol would have to measure himself against such established favourites as Musard and Dufresne with their far larger orchestras, and against a young man called Offenbach, whom some critics already suspected of being able to eclipse him.

He made a successful progress via Munich, Ulm, Stuttgart, and Strasburg, and reached the French capital when winter had already set in (October 27th). In Paris they had a whole Hotel to themselves, and as the weather was very cold Strauss was put to a great deal of extra expense providing wood for the fires. He stayed there from November until April, winning golden opinions from all the musicians of the day, from Auber, Cherubini, Meyerbeer, Berlioz. He gave a series of brilliant concerts, supplied the music for all the important society balls of the season, and performed at the Tuileries before Louis Philippe and his Court.[1] Later he extended his tour throughout some of the French provincial cities,[2] and then to Belgium and the Netherlands. In order to keep his orchestra in good humour despite the tremendous exactions of so much travel and so much work, Strauss was obliged to "do" them exceptionally well. The expenses of the tour ran away with the great bulk of all he was able to earn. Little enough money made its way back either to the house in the Kumpfgasse, or to poor Frau Anna. Nevertheless Johann's musicians were so homesick by the time he proposed to proceed to England as to be on the verge of mutiny. They found Paris dazzling,

[1] Next day he received 2,000 francs and a diamond pin.
[2] Xmas in Rouen, conducting the music for a ball which lasted until four in the morning.

E

but strange and foreign; they were longing for the home comforts of Vienna. Not a man among them but would have exchanged the most elaborate table d'hôte for a dish of "Beuschel" and dumplings. It was only because of the disgrace or difficulties consequent on any breach of contract that they decided to carry on at all.

Strauss did his utmost to hold the band together, and to hearten his companions with the same dream of the riches to be come by in London, which danced before him like a Will-o'-the-Wisp and nerved his own overstrained organism to further and further exertions. We can imagine an exotic enough little group of dispirited expatriated Viennese musicians shivering on the deck of an early—very early—Victorian cross-channel steamer and landing in a sea-fret at Dover,[1] wretched beyond words! They wore top hats and loud checked trousers. With their swarthy looks and jaundiced sea-sick faces they must have struck the "unsympathetisch" barbarians on that bleak quayside as a very "furrin" looking crew indeed. They, for their part, had come to an appalling country where there was no wit, no wine, no warmth, no sun, no gaiety, and no understanding for music!

Strauss and Hirsch had all their work cut out to counteract this devastating disaffection. Johann had no gift for leadership except at the conductor's desk, and suffered acutely himself from every ill which beset his companions.

At first everything in England fell out in most disastrous fashion. The accommodation which had been bespoken in London beforehand from Paris turned out to be very unsatisfactory, and the orchestra found itself obliged to bundle summarily out of some Todger-like Hotel and seek lodgings elsewhere. The proprietor, however, demanded full compensation from the luckless Viennese strangers, and while

[1] April 11th, 1838.

Strauss was out and about one day, trying to arrange matters, a thief broke into his room and laid hands on all the ready money he could find. Things went from bad to worse. Unable to patch up this hotel business, or indeed, to meet his expenses at all, now, Strauss found himself likely to be committed to an English prison for debt. Shade of Dickens, the Marshalsea, or of the King's Bench! It would have needed the creator of "Little Dorrit" indeed to describe his plight and his despair. . . .

Fortunately, however, England was not so sunk in indifference to art as people abroad believed, nor was there wanting someone in London who knew what a Strauss waltz meant. A Mr. Cock, a music publisher, came forward and suggested a way out of these hideous embarrassments and complications. Herr Strauss should write something for him and matters could doubtless be arranged. . . .

At first Johann feared his obligations towards his Viennese publisher might militate against this solution of his troubles, but Mr. Cock assured him he could and would deal successfully with Herr Haslinger, if only the desired waltz were produced. Strauss might muddle his finances, come to grief in a strange unfriendly city, get into trouble with his musikers, but when it came to writing a waltz——!

The piece instantly flowed from his ready pen, and his troubles were banished. Mr. Cock knew his business, and achieved a hit with the bewitching novelty. Johann found himself in funds again and set about arranging his first London concert.

This was not too well attended, but the press notices were so good that the second concert was sold out at once. Thus, for instance, spoke *The Times* for April 18th,— "This celebrated composer of waltzes arrived here with his band on Thursday last and gave a concert at the Hanover Square rooms yesterday evening. The pieces performed were chiefly his own waltzes, but they are done in a manner most extraordinary and altogether novel in this country. He has so completely trained his band to work with him that all separate individuality is lost, and effect is produced like that of an accurately constructed machine, the most eccentric instruments such as bells, castanets, cracking whips, etc., are occasionally introduced, and the construction of many pieces is highly fantastic, yet never is the mechanical precision lost for an instant. Thus the band, though small, is made to give the effect of one three times more numerous. From the immense fame which Herr Strauss has acquired in Vienna, a more numerous audience might have been expected than attended on this occasion. The smallness of this audience is chiefly to be attributed to the very inefficient means which were taken to give the public notice of the concert, as well as the injudicious selection of an opera night.

"However, Herr Strauss can hardly fail to attract in the long run, as he and his band fully deserve all the fame they have acquired on the continent."

The *Musical World* wrote of "The First Concert of Mr. Strauss" in a truly Victorian vein:

"Shall we confess that we are too old to dance? So is the fact, but let not the gentle reader imagine that if our bodily frame be feeble, the intellectual faculty is not instantly stimulated by the sounds of the exhilarating quadrille or the voluptuous waltz. Verily, we delight in, and feel ourselves young at the sight of these exercises, we revel in the overflowing of kind and generous feelings, and ever does the first note from the brilliant orchestra come rushing upon our minds in all the freshness of juvenile emotion—Who has not heard of Strauss, the Croesus of waltz composers —he who scours round the continent and returns home ten thousand pounds the richer man? We were not a little

anxious to meet the modern Midas, and it was with no
ordinary feelings of interest that we entered the Hanover
Square rooms on Tuesday last, to hear his introductory
concert. But there was something cold, comfortless and
formal in the *tout ensemble*, when we thought on the gay
promenades, the ottomans, the fountains encircled with
rare and glowing exotics, the café, with its troops of perfumed
waiters, which so steal away the senses in the Rue Saint
Honoré, of which Musard is the divinity and ruling power.
The appearance of M. Strauss and his fellow-labourers in
the vineyard of Terpsichore soon, however, dissipated these
emotions. His is not the waltz which steals over the senses
with a warm and voluptuous feeling; on the contrary, it
speaks out imperatively of the girding up of loins, the bracing
of sinews, and the never-tiring elasticity of vigorous limbs.
"The following was the bill of fare:—

Part I. Overture du Serment, Auber;
Le Philomelen Valse, Strauss;
Introduction & Variations for the Flute, composed
and executed by Robert Frisch;
Les Bouquets, Strauss.

Part II. La Gabrielle Valse, Strauss;
Rondo for the Oboe, executed by Mr. Bamberg;
Mosaic of Waltzes, by Strauss;
The Telegrafe Musicale, a grand Pot Pourri, Strauss.

"As a composer and arranger, M. Strauss has evinced
throughout these movements great tact and considerable
originality. His strength lies in an ingenuity of detail, a
striking brilliancy, strong colouring, and extreme contrasts.
In the place of the elegant solo on the violin, the gentle
remonstrance of the oboe, the full tide of affection from the
clarionet, the tale of passion from the upper strings of the
violoncello—features which so distinguish the orchestra
in the ballet of Her Majesty's Theatre—we have a

spirit-stirring combination of horns, trumpets, trombones, ophicleides, and other instruments of a loud and sonorous character. In fact, the score is an amalgamation of brass instruments, occasionally relieved by the stringed and wind bands. But they are well put together; and if their frequent use takes away the feeling of repose and refinement, it excites an energy and vividness of sensation, which is perhaps no less agreeable and enchanting.

"In his melodies he displays much clearness of design, and great boldness of outline. The disposition of his brass band is generally novel, frequently clever, and always claims attention. Of the wood band we cannot say so much; and the stringed band appears scarcely powerful enough to make its way through the other instruments.

"The performance of his music is most remarkable for precision and unanimity of sentiment; and the contrasts come out in an extraordinary manner. In these respects the band of M. Strauss is assuredly unequalled."

Again, "we can boast of professors who can do all that M. Strauss has done with the waltz, but we have no band, which is so completely under the sway and subjugation of the conductor—no small orchestra which can produce so vivid and exciting an impression."

Again, on Saturday, May 12th, 1838 an account appeared in the papers of a grand ball at Buckingham Palace, the first State Ball since Queen Victoria's accession, at which Strauss appeared. "A temporary stage for Strauss' Waltz Band was fitted up on the south side of the ballroom, as the regular orchestra only afforded accommodation for eighteen musicians. . . . The Band performed Strauss' entire new set of waltzes entitled 'Hommage à la Reine d'Angleterre', which were much admired by Her Majesty." Thus the *Court Gazette*.

Strauss and his orchestra were indispensable, of course,

at a great ball given in the course of this brilliant season, at the Russian Embassy. The arrangements were such, however, that the Viennese master and his musicians had to clamber up a ladder and through a window to reach the place set apart for the band.

They played at Almack's and Willis' Rooms, in The City of London Tavern, and in a dozen other well-known fashionable resorts.

From London the Viennese orchestra went on to Birmingham and Liverpool and Manchester and Dublin.

Strauss was to some degree intoxicated with his success[1] in England. He gave concerts all over the country, at Birmingham, Leamington, Bath, Southampton, Brighton, Portsmouth. His ambition soared. He began to entertain the idea of still wider realms to conquer! He proposed, now, to go to America. But his orchestra would not listen to the project for one moment. Strauss' personal laurels were not necessarily theirs; and, if his double household in Vienna offered him no particular temptation to return, they at least could bear their "Heimweh" no more. They could scarcely endure the English climate a day longer, nor the English cooking! Once more their Leader was at his wits' end how to induce them to fulfil the innumerable engagements and contracts to which he was continually committing himself. He reasoned and argued and cajoled as best such a choleric, temperamental man might do such things, and only at last succeeded in getting his musicians to remain with him a while longer under promises of increased pay, and an immediate flight to the south of France. The latter expedient, however, did not help him very much. He soon found himself forced to return to England under threat of every sort of trouble if he failed to fulfil his contracts and pledges there. Back then they all went, these mutinous

[1] He often received as much as £200 a night.

Viennese, dragged by the fiery Director not merely through fifteen cities of early Victorian England, through Reading, Cheltenham, Worcester, Leicester, Sheffield, Derby, but even north to Scotland, where they played at Edinburgh and Glasgow.[1]

There they had many adventures including the overturning of one of the post coaches in which they were travelling on a snowy mountain road, when it was only by the united, and doubtless very shiftless, exertions of the whole company, under the incomprehensible directions of the Scotch driver, that a fallen horse was saved from rolling over the precipice.

The Scotch Sabbath suited the Austrian musicians in no way at all. They fell foul of it, and of their dour-faced landlords in Edinburgh and elsewhere, on every occasion. At last they turned southward again *en route* for Dover and the Continent, playing at Newcastle, Leeds, Hull, Wakefield and other places.

Strauss himself was utterly worn out. He collapsed at a concert at Leicester, and fell seriously ill as soon as they got to Calais. His nerves could stand no more, and a high fever set in. A Parisian doctor who happened to be on hand gave it as his opinion that the Herr Direktor should have at least a month's complete rest before he attempted to proceed any further.

The *Musical World* in England thus told the story:

"Strauss' Last Waltz

"The hero of the Waltz lies stretched on the bed of sickness at Calais—'Alas! how changed from him,' etc. We would we had the neat hand at the parody of a verse, which belongs to some of our distinguished readers—we should

[1] For a much more detailed account of Strauss' British tour the reader should consult Herr Lange's "Josef Lanner and Johann Strauss" published by Messrs. Breitkopf and Härtel, Leipzig.

then no longer be embarrassed to conclude our quotation
with 'that soul of *limb*;' an appellation of peculiar felicity,
we flatter ourselves, in the instance of the celebrated dancing
musician Strauss.

"As the hour of sickness is held to be a good time for the
inculcation of a little morality, we shall, after the manner
of the most orthodox divines, endeavour to *improve* the
occasion, by a word of advice, (which is at present much
needed), to those who are disposed to make money too
fast, and damage their constitutions, their fame, and
worst of all—music itself, by a horrid greediness after the
receipts of concerts. 'Be warned in time, ye itinerant
speculators,' observe what we shall say of the fate of Strauss,
and tremble.

"Modern times have produced some great men, the short-
ness of whose career was perhaps more than compensated
by its brilliancy. Bonaparte, Lord Byron and, shall we
add, Strauss? are examples of this . . .

"To have set all the crowned heads of Europe in motion,
and universally harmonized the attitudes of beauty, is
one of the least glories of Strauss. From the elevation of
his orchestra, with the calmness of an Apollo, all the live-
long night he has looked on at our mortal pleasures—he
has seen empires nodding to their fall'—enamoured kings,
and probably enraptured *queans*, but what of that? His
glory is in having interfused his own soul into those of a
set of followers so perfectly, that even in dance music they
have given a lesson to the best orchestras of Europe. Strauss
is legion,—forty mortal, or rather spiritual existences,
hang upon his, and must dissolve with his last breath.
Of how much value the life of him who operates on the
hearts of some—the heels of all!

"Strauss was first in jeopardy in Paris. Driving home in
a fog from a ball between night and morning, like Falstaff,

'hissing hot,' his cabriolet was nearly driven into the Seine and turned into a bathing machine. Escaped from this perilous refreshment, he came to England, realised immense sums in London, and while he stayed there did well, because he got his regular morning sleep. But there was no way of annihilating time and space in the country —there were no griffins or hippogriffs kept at livery stables to transfer our Comus and his whole rout of companions to the next ball in time for them to get rest—they were compelled to put up with a very unpoetical stage coach. But what with playing all night and travelling all day— what with concerts in the morning and balls in the evening, travelling post haste here, and grasping at a fresh engagement there, catching cold without leisure to attend to it, and sleeping on no consideration whatever, the whole party became so utterly jaded, knocked up, and incapable, that there is probably not a man of them but will remember England as long as he lives.

"As for Strauss, who is on his bed at Calais, he finds himself very successful, much applauded, rich—and dying."

Then, later:

"Since writing, we have not heard any fatal news of Strauss. If by any chance he should rec ver—we shall not permit such an accident to spoil the *mural* of our biography—and enter our protest accordingly."

Fortunately Strauss did not die.

But his serious illness, and the consequent delay meant the disbanding of his orchestra. Despite the disagreements and dissensions of the tour, every one of his musicians regretted such an end to it as this. They would have even consented, now, to carry on together yet awhile if only "der Alte" might recover. But they had little alternative. One by one they regretfully took leave of the sick and broken man, laden only with his greeting to Vienna, and to the "Old Stefferl."

Only Reichmann, the clarinettist, remained behind with Strauss. It fell to his lot later to get the sick man home. This, too, was a difficult and risky business. Johann was quite unfit to travel, especially in the comfortless coaches of that period, sheltered from draughts and cold only by his own rugs, and by what packing of trampled straw the various posting houses could provide. At Strasburg he suffered such a serious relapse that his life itself seemed to be in danger. Reichmann watched beside him day and night. He lay tossing in delirium only to come to himself weaker than ever, and to implore his companion to take to the road again, come what might. It was not before the weary pair reached Linz and the Austrian frontier that Strauss revived at all.

At long long last they came to the final stage of this nightmare of a journey. It seemed, indeed, to have been planned under an unlucky star. Even as the sick man, broken in mind and body, came in sight of the well loved city which he had left so full of purpose and high hope nearly two years before, the post horses bolted and an accident nearly cost him his life.

A group of his friends had come as far as Purkersdorf, the last posting station before Vienna, to greet him. They brought him back about eight o'clock, and Frau Anna, who had been fetched from a visit to the Theatre, was shocked, like everybody else, at his condition.

He was in a state of high fever. Nevertheless, here he was again home in Vienna! They put him to bed and for four weeks the doctors, two of them, gave him their utmost care.

Strauss slowly recovered . . . and began to think in terms of concerts again.

At no time in his life was the contrast greater than now between his private and his public circumstances.

In the Hirschenhaus Frau Anna was nursing a man back to health who had almost ceased to be any husband to her. She knew all about the pretty spendthrift girl he was keeping just across the river. She knew well enough what fabulous sums of money he was said to have earned all over the continent, and in far away rich England, but if she had ever received five hundred gulden a month for her housekeeping and the education of Schani and Pepperl and the rest, it was as much as she ever saw, while that woman in the Kumpfgasse flaunted the most ridiculous clothes. . . .

For the public, now, Strauss was second in importance only to the Emperor. The city had two idols, Ferdinand and Johann.

It has not often been the lot of a musician to receive full recognition in his own day. Beethoven and Schubert never knew the popularity of Strauss. The Waltz King had attained his zenith. Vienna went wild with joy when he was able to make his appearance again after so long an absence and so severe an illness.

A tremendous evening was arranged to welcome him once more, at the Sperl. He wrote some special music for the occasion and introduced the new dance from Paris, the Quadrille, which had taken his fancy there so much, that he had sometimes relinquished the Conductor's desk at the great balls in the Rue St. Honoré to take his place in Dufresne's orchestra and study it from that practical point of vantage. The enthusiasm at the Sperl was indescribable. Strauss conducted the whole evening, and wept at the reception his dear Vienna gave him there, as Vienna wept with joy to see him back.

From then on the city danced its shoes into holes again every night.

It suited the statecraft of Metternich to keep Vienna at once supine and intoxicated. Only thus could democratic ideas or social discontents be smothered or held at bay. The popular god at whose feet the city lay was a fanatical devotee of the Emperor and of the system—or rather the House—he represented. Strauss was no politician. He used to say he had no time to bother his head with politics, and in any case it was not equal to them. He might equally well have said it was not safe to do so! He stuck to his fiddle bow. As long as Vienna danced, the threatenings and rumblings of political and financial discontent could be masked. Prince Metternich in the Imperial Chancellory knew well enough that "the System" trembled on the edge of an abyss, but so long as Strauss fiddled, the witchery of it held a thousand threats at bay. Hence the welcome from rich and poor, high and low alike, to the Master on his home-coming.

But at home in the Hirschenhaus, and in the Kumpfgasse, it was a different story. There Strauss was poor, and more irritable than ever.

As time went on, and children began to be born to Emilie Trampusch, the breach between Johann and his wife was complete. Nothing could bridge it again. The Hofball-musikdirektor definitely turned his back on his legitimate home at last, and took himself off to live with Emilie. This was in 1845.

Not that he had much money to spare even for his irregular ménage. The pair had a rather shabby apartment in the Andraschen Haus, not far from the Hirschenhaus, but just across the Danube Canal.

Strauss' room, choked up with a lot of old-fashioned furniture, a piano which also served as a writing-desk, a number of bird-cages, had only one window in it. Strauss was fond of animals. He kept a dog which sometimes accompanied him on his tours, and two little monkeys.

In the course of time four unfortunate little girls were born in the Kumpfgasse, Emeline, Klementine, Marie, and Theresa, and one son Johann.[1] And it was here, in this tall dark house up a narrow alley facing a blank wall like a prison, that the idol of Vienna lived the last few years of an outwardly and publicly successful life. It was here eventually he died.

Frau Strauss, left in the Hirschenhaus, bore the scandal of it, and the bitterness as best she might, in silence.

She turned with her whole heart to her children, and especially to Schani.

[1] Fritz Lange in *Josef Lanner and Johann Strauss*, gives a brief epitome of what happened eventually to Johann the Second's pitiful group of half-sisters and the brother. They fell into misery. The son was a weakling; he died at twenty-nine. The eldest girl tried the stage without success. The poor child, through whom the father caught his dying sickness, was so atrociously mishandled by the mother, and beaten, that she had to be sent to a Home. She ran away and came back to Vienna where some good Nuns took care of her. She eked out an insufficient living as an artificial flower-maker. Later when the wonderful half-brother of these poor waifs became a rich and successful man he did a good deal to help them. But what an irony it all was!

When is some playwright going to give us these poignant contrasts (to an intoxicating accompaniment of Strauss music) on the stage? Surely they offer human "stuff" enough!

CHAPTER VI

SCHANI'S DÉBUT, '44

ONCE the father had left the house, nothing more stood in the way of the young Johann pushing forward his studies for all he was worth. The support and education of the family devolved upon the deserted wife, but otherwise "a nightmare had vanished". Apparently Strauss senior now contributed nothing to the Hirschenhaus ménage, for in six months' time it became necessary for "Schani" to keep his mother's head above water.

First of all he put in some serious work with the violin under Kohlmann, Director of the Ballet at the Kärntnertor Theatre. Then came counterpoint and theory under two men of considerable eminence, Professors Hoffmann and Drechsler.

The latter was exactly the right man for Johann, a sworn enemy to innovation and to the taking of musical liberties. Although quite a successful secular composer, ecclesiastical music engrossed his best energies, and he was Choir Master at one of the principal churches in Vienna.

He formed a high opinion of his new pupil's abilities, and attempted to turn his gifts in the direction of Church music. Johann seems to have made attempts at writing Introits and Kyries, but somewhat different rhythms stuck obstinately in that curly dark head. On one occasion after a solemn session at the organ, the youth only waited to satisfy himself that the church door was shut, to indulge in a lively polka.

Drechsler broke now and again into an access of despair over one or another of Johann's technical weaknesses, and roundly declared that he would never amount to anything!

Nevertheless at the end he wrote him a glowing and encouraging testimonial which sufficed, together with a respectable "Gradual" of the youth's own composition, to obtain for Johann at the hands of the civic authorities the necessary license to direct an orchestra. He was disappointed though, for like all the more serious-minded musicians of the time, he held dance music as an unworthy outcome of contrapuntal study.

"Go away," he grumbled, "and scribble jigs like your father. You didn't need me for that."

Johann was still a minor, only nineteen. The magistrate waived this point in his favour, and also that of the father's consent to his son's career. At the beginning of September, 1844, he received the necessary permit to set out in life for himself.

Another month went by and Johann had scratched up an orchestra of twenty-four members. Strings and wind were always to be found where unemployed geniuses forgathered at an inn called "Zur Stadt Belgrade". After a mere six months of previous study his art demanded hectic practising now, and the new conductor worked tremendously hard to get his repertory together. At the beginning of October all was ready for the great adventure. Johann had provided himself with four waltzes, two quadrilles, three polkas; otherwise he had little with which to make his bow to Vienna but self-confident ambition, and a very famous name.

.   .   .   .   .

The Dommayerbau at Hietzing[1] was a festive resort in Vienna, at once dance-hall, concert-hall, and restaurant,

[1] To-day the Park Hotel has been built upon this site.

only a little less fashionable and pretentious than the
famous Sperl and Apollosaal.

With a vivid historical imagination one can easily
visualise the excitement here on a certain amazing evening
in October, 1844, nearly a hundred years ago, when all
Vienna, animated with devouring curiosity and every sort
of laughingly malicious anticipation, flocked to the Dommayerbau as if it were the only attraction in the city.

The occasion of this unparalleled concourse was a public
announcement which had appeared but two days previously.
It was an invitation to a soirée dansante at Dommayer's
Casino, in which Johann Strauss Junior would have the
honour to direct his own orchestra for the first time, and
to produce some of his own compositions together with
various Overtures and numbers from the Operas. It respect-
fully solicited the patronage of the public, and proposed to
commence at six o'clock.

It fell on the city, on the populous Hirschenhaus, and
certainly in the shabby apartment across the river, like a bolt
from the blue. True, the appearance of a new "Kapelle"
was nothing in itself, but this one meant that a rival had
started up to the uncrowned King of Vienna, and that
in no less a person than his own son! The sensation was
immense. All the father's partisans were up in arms. The
musical critics in the papers were none too kindly disposed
to the bold young man. The entire Kaiserstadt hung on the
event, consumed with the liveliest anticipations.

Public affairs were in a bad way; revolution was smoul-
dering throughout the Empire; extremes of poverty and
luxury made a scandal in the capital—but still Vienna
danced. As we have stated before, it suited Authority
and Metternich that society should dance; only thus could
it be kept oblivious of the chasms yawning everywhere in
the fabric of the Habsburg State.

F

Vienna was quite willing to dance. The announcement of Schani's début thrilled the city to the exclusion of all other topics. This rivalry to the Waltz King starting up in the bosom of his own family promised a sensation which no one, high or low, was willing to miss. People who had money for nothing else somehow or other found enough to go to Dommayer's that evening.

Long before the entertainment was to begin, quite indeed by five o'clock in the afternoon, the great Mariahilf and Schönbrunn streets were as thronged with people and with equipages setting off for Dommayer's as if it had been a public holiday. Every sort of fashionable high-wheeled two-seater driven by the sparks of the day was to be seen manœuvring for the advantage of the road with family conveyances of more solid style, and with the packed Zieselwagen which would have been besieged and boarded in the Inner City. Away they all bumped over the cobbles with their drivers in blue coats, knee breeches, and tall top hats, no less excited at the prospect of this famous début than their laughing, chattering, disputing passengers.

At Hietzing the crush was so great, that a jam was formed at the entrance to the Gardens. Dommayer's had never seen anything like it. It was only with the utmost difficulty that one could fight one's way through. The police got nasty when important individuals made too free with their elbows. Women got hurt, and fainted. At the Casino doors the police had rather more than they could do to control the press and extricate people on foot from the confusion of the carriages.

Within, every table was besieged, and the waiters could scarcely move! People sat and perspired, grumbled about the air, damned the arrangements in general, got rattled about the delay, but nevertheless stuck "bumfest" to their places.

The ballroom at Dommayer's was a fanciful place, with slender columns, an ornamental stucco ceiling and gorgeous chandeliers. The scene must have largely resembled many a gay and popular gathering at the Vauxhall Gardens in early nineteenth-century London—given, of course, the crystalline Viennese atmosphere. No matter whoever else had or had not contrived to get a seat at Dommayer's that evening, partisans of Strauss Père were there in full force, resolved to make some sort of a demonstration on the least possible excuse. Lampenhirsch himself and the publisher Haslinger were there, hoping to sit over a good glass of wine listening to a few thoroughly second-rate dance tunes, and to witness a failure which would once and for all scotch this danger of a formidable family rivalry. Strauss Père himself had strenuously refused to attend the occasion.

Far removed, again, in a remote corner, unnoticed, sat a quiet little woman with a keen observant face. Perhaps it was confident . . . perhaps it betrayed anxiety. . . . Whatever had been her sufferings in the past Schani's mother sat and prayed this evening that his début would compensate for them all, and justify her for the stand she had made to let this ambitious brilliant boy of hers go his own way.

Johann the younger himself, behind the scenes, was got up to kill. But even his wonderful new coat of finest blue cloth with silver buttons, and his gorgeous silk waistcoat covered with hand-embroidered flowers (all as yet unpaid for) could not still the suffocating beating of his heart. He was sick with "Lampenfieber" (stage fright), chalk white, and scourged with that anticipation of spectacular failure which was to beset him at a première all his fabulously successful life.

The orchestra began tuning up, and a hush fell throughout the hall. It was Schani's zero hour. Next moment he had to go over the top. . . .

He appeared, dark, arresting, slender. A storm of applause greeted the bowing young figure. Aware of the forest of faces before him, and of the mass emotion, friendly and unfriendly, centred upon him, Strauss turned quickly, tapped his violin sharply with the bow, and began. . . .

The Overture "Die Stumme von Portici" was well but not rapturously received. The orchestra was too small to do it justice. But this was neither here nor there.

With the first bars of a new piece called the "Gunstwerber",[1] a waltz of his own composition, began the great experiment of the evening. The audience sat suddenly spell-bound and entranced, keen and instantly alive to the newness, the freshness, the individuality and charm of this melody. This was what they had been led to hope for and expect, what they had flocked to Dommayer's to hear. A new star had indeed arisen in the Viennese firmament, and the rapturous applause which greeted the spirited finale of the dance sufficiently showed that it had made an immediate hit. People stood up on the chairs and waved their hands and handkerchiefs, they cheered and clapped, and shouted, pressing forward tumultuously in their eagerness to reach the platform, overturning tables everywhere in their heedless wake. Dommayer's was in an uproar of enthusiasm!

The ovation went to Schani's head, banishing his diffidence on the instant, and investing him from head to foot with that pythian-vibration, fire and elasticity, with which he was henceforth to conduct his orchestras all over the world.

He bowed, bowed repeatedly, his face no longer white, but red and glowing, his black eyes flashing and snapping like live coals. Then he turned again and swiftly signalled an encore.

[1] Like me!

The next waltz delighted the audience still more. It had to be given five times. Dommayer's became a scene of indescribable enthusiasm, the yells for an encore repeated on all sides seemed as if they would never subside. Young Strauss, beaming with joy and self-confidence, raises his violin again, and sets it to his chin. His eyes are shining with something more than the intoxication of this incredible triumph . . . it is no composition of his own this time which he deigns to give this seething audience, but the majestic "Lorelei Rheinklänge" by his father . . . Vienna understands the gesture. Women break into tears, and here and there even the men's eyes are wet. This was "Alt" Strauss's finest piece, the thing identified with all he had come to mean in the life of the Kaiserstadt, and the son is playing it now perhaps as it had never been played before, as an act, in his own supreme hour, of filial esteem and public acknowledgement. How he plays it too! The same charm and matchless dexterity as the father's, the same poise and verve.

Three more original pieces followed, his "Sinngedichte", "Début-Quadrille", "Herzenslust Polka", and Strauss' son, had captured his audience. Applause echoed to the roof. The pieces were called for over and over again, and over and over again the sheer magic of melody and hectic tune held the audience spell-bound. Then they broke into frantic ovations . . . the son was acclaimed every whit as great as his father.

If the poor mother who had been through so much, taking her son in her arms behind the scenes, could weep for joy, the father's faction made their crestfallen way out of the press, wondering how "der Alte" would take it. Hirsch had no idea how he was to break this sort of news to his bosom friend waiting up for him in the Andraschen house. Would it throw Johann senior into a passion, or reconcile him with Schani? On the whole Hirsch decided to sleep over the matter . . . perhaps the notices in the papers in the morning would do something to help him out.

The critics had been sitting all the evening through in the densest of the crush at Dommayer's. Vogt, for one, had been able to get nothing to eat. The waiters lost their heads and were run off their feet. The great man was so pushed and knocked about that at length he could stand no more, so fought his way outside for a breath of fresh air. Once free of the worst of the press he jotted down his notes for the morning paper.

"Talent is the monopoly of no single individual . . . it can be transmitted . . . this young man is fully as melodious, as piquant, as effective in his instrumentation as his father . . . nevertheless he is no slavish imitator of the latter's methods of composition".

This from an important pressman who went supperless to bed after an exhausting evening, must be held to be praise indeed.

Herr Wiest, feuilletonist of the "Wanderers", drove home past Lanner's in a cab. Involuntarily he waved his hand, "Good night, Lanner! Good evening, Father Strauss! Good morning to you, Strauss junior!"

Champagne, of course, had been flowing at Dommayer's. Schani must receive the congratulations of his special friends, and of the perspiring, overwhelmed proprietor. It was nearly three o'clock in the morning before the youthful Kapellmeister and his mother took their seats in a hackney carriage to drive back to Vienna.

The printing shops of the news sheets of the day were all lit up and busy with the reports to be broadcast over the city by breakfast time.

Four nights after this enthusiastic and eventful affair, Johann fulfilled an engagement in Semmering, and then

JOHANN STRAUSS, SOHN.

played again at Dommayer's. One or two appearances
sufficed to establish his name. All the proprietors of dance
and pleasure resorts in Vienna who had hitherto depended
upon Strauss senior as an unfailing draw, now found it in
the interests of business to boom and advertise this amazing
son. Everywhere people scanned the Strauss placards and
announcements now to see whether it was to be "Vater"
or "Sohn".

The young director of the new orchestra had made a
spectacular hit. He was immediately bombarded with
engagements, and within the shortest possible space of
time conquered both the Outer and the Inner City. All
sorts of romantic and fantastic stories flew from lip to
lip about him—one that he had been in love with a maiden,
Reserl Struber, from boyhood, and had played to her as
she died. This was entirely in keeping with the type of
his success, and served most appropriately to heighten it.

As for the elder Strauss, he found himself possessed in
a night of a famous son. It remained for him to decide
what to do about it—whether to resent and fear this rival
and usurper of a "Schani", or whether to acknowledge
with secret pride that that boy had indeed made good!
The fame of a dance-band leader might perhaps last as
long as that of the dance, and how long was the life of a
waltz? Thirty years? Hummel had once been modern,
as had Lanner, as had he himself—but a new artist had
now appeared who outstripped them all. The day went to
his son, and after a while the father was ready to
acknowledge it.

The young man had no mind to thrust his father
musically into the shade. He had ever held his artistry
in the highest estimation, and in the hour of his own glowing
triumph, when abundant success assured prosperity to
the mother who had borne the brunt of so much of the

fighting, "Schani" made the rightful gesture. He wanted to be happy, and that others, especially those shipwrecked parents, should be happy too. So he placed works of the elder Strauss foremost in his programmes, especially at the Dommayer, and this emphatically because he found in them what it was he loved and admired in his father. "It was no theatrical flourish," says Decsey, "but an innate longing after harmony."

The youth wrote a letter to his father explaining his reasons for taking his mother's side in the sad business of their estrangement, which would be laughable because of its terrifically long-winded pompous diction, were it not sincerely touching. It loses tremendously in translation. In the original, one sentence, with immense circumlocutions couched in forms of the utmost respect and ceremony, comprises the major part of the letter. Young Johann conserved a very real affection for his father right up to the end, together with an unfeigned admiration for him as a musician, both as composer and executant. He seems to have borne no sort of grudge for the harshnesses of his own childhood, nor to have cherished any rancour over the fact that every obstacle possible had been put in the way of his choosing his own career. These things were forgotten, but his mother's wrongs remained. Johann's loyalty to Frau Anna was the only criticism of his father that he allowed himself. He took upon himself the burden of the deserted family with a heart that ached as much for them as for the paternal truant, and through the intervening time before a "unilateral" reconcilement came about, he was torn between the happiness of freedom at last and the desire for a thorough understanding with his father.

Strauss senior evidently understood this letter. They met, the father and son, and talked much out together. Misunderstandings were cleared away. The bitterness wrought by gossip and scandalmongering was allayed, and a reconciliation as far as they two were concerned was sealed with hand clasps and tobacco. But there still remained a problem Schani could not solve, the problem of the deserted wife, and the mistress.

Johann could not and would not desert his mother, but his father could find no way back to her. Otherwise they might have joined musical forces, Schani, as natural second in command, and first violin in his parent's orchestra. This arrangement would indeed obviate any appearance of enmity and rivalry for the future. But it would have been treachery to the family in the Hirschenhaus, and without occasioning offence, Johann managed to decline his father's offer. They came to an amicable agreement, each to pursue his own way, competitors of course, but friendly ones, and loyal. Strauss senior was to be found, henceforth, at the Sperl, at Zeisigs, and at the "Sieben Kürfursten", Strauss junior at Dommayer's, at Zum Grünen Tore at Zogernitz . . .

Both had their followers. Never in our own days could idolised film star boast of more fanatical fans than those who ranged themselves under these two flags.

Moreover, both musicians directed a military orchestras, as well as dozens of civil ones.

Lanner, who died in 1843, had been Band Master to the 2nd Bürger regiment. On his death Strauss junior had received this appointment. His father directed the Band of the 1st Bürger regiment. They sported somewhat similar uniforms—both looked rakish and well in the high shako. Should these bands happen to encounter each other in the streets or squares of the city they halted, saluted, did a right-about-turn, and smartly marched off in opposite directions. The manœuvre required considerable dexterity in some of the narrow ways of old Vienna!

Complications, however, were automatically avoided when Strauss senior took himself abroad. He departed on another concert tour to Prussia, and later to England again. In 1845 he attained the zenith of his ambition, and the highest point of his outwardly successful career in being appointed Director to the Ball Music at Court. He conducted at many a brilliant assembly in the beautiful Redoutensaal. This was a far more tasteful ballroom than any at the Sperl. It was situated in the vast pile of the Hofburg itself between the Schweizerhof and the summer Riding School on the one hand, and the open Josefsplatz on the other. " It was a long hall in the late baroque style in which 600 people could be seated. The walls were covered to a height of six feet with finest Gobelin tapestries. Above these, against cool panelling picked out in gold, embellished with every conceivable device of gilded ornament, were long mirrors reflecting and counter-reflecting all the formal elegance made dazzling by the brilliance from the crystal chandeliers suspended from the gilded ceiling. At one end there was a sort of stage . . . backed by a decorated sweep of wall which continued the line of the mouldings above the tapestries, and this was broken by a branching staircase, scarlet carpeted, forming a sort of balcony which was opened on to by tall double doors high above the level of the stage."[1]

Strange it is to think that the visitor wandering through Vienna to-day can still visit a scene like this, in which nothing now could recall the faintest echo of that bewitching melody and gaiety of which it was once the setting. . .!

Johann junior never cared much at any time to leave Vienna. But it became imperative for him to undertake a few tours. His reputation, and that of his orchestra, demanded it. He presently went off to the Balkans where all sorts of success and all sorts of amusing adventures

[1] " *Vienna* " E. Crankshaw.

befell him. When he appeared in the uniform of the
Viennese "Bürgergarde" the people were immensely impressed. In Belgrade a Turkish Pasha took him for some
vastly important Austrian big-wig and accorded him the
highest military honours. On the other hand, in one queer
place—Pancsova—his fame had so little preceded him that
his instruments were publicly confiscated, and he had some
comical difficulty about redeeming them in Kronstadt.

At a certain town elsewhere, being again mistaken for
some high plenipotentiary, a deputation of worthies waited
upon him, requiring him to have some local authority,
an unpopular individual, removed. Strauss had no time
or patience to get this business straightened out, so he
made an acceptable pretence of acceding to this demand—
for which bit of tomfoolery he was called to account on his
return to Vienna.

CHAPTER VII

REVOLUTION IN VIENNA '48

MEANWHILE Johann the Younger was busily writing. Dance after dance came from his pen. The waltz he dedicated to Jenny Lind in the summer of 1846, when the Swedish nightingale caused a furore in Vienna, brought the number of these compositions since his début at the Dommayer Casino ten months previously, up to one and twenty. Of these some were written for his regiment, and others, on his tour, for the Serbs and the Czechs.

Clouds were gathering, however, not only far and wide all over the far-flung political horizon of the Empire, but ever more and more darkly over Vienna itself. While society danced and flirted and revelled in its chosen palaces to an unending succession of fresh fantasies from Johann, bakers' shops were being raided and plundered by desperate people in the poor parts of the city. Things everywhere were in a very bad way. People from whom the taxes could only be collected by military threat, would pawn their watches for a ticket to the Sperl or the Sofiensaal. All quarters of the city swarmed with beggars and prostitutes. King Louis Philippe, who had recently visited it, expressed his amazement that no revolution broke out. Terrific disorders were indeed on the point of explosion. But the Kaiserstadt, sick of a thousand fevers and ulcers—still danced.

It will be necessary here to sketch in the kaleidoscopic political background of the next few hectic months. While the two Johann Strausses set the whole thing to music, Austria went up in flames.

In 1848 revolution, encouraged by example elsewhere, by famine, by crushing oppression and exploitation of the people, broke out from one end of the Habsburg Empire to the other, in Milan, Venice, Vienna, Bohemia and Hungary. Marshal Radetzky, commander of the Imperial Forces in Italy, triumphed over Charles Albert of Piedmont, at Custozza, in July, and was given a tremendous reception on his return to Vienna.

But previous to this, on March 13th, the uproar in the city brought about the downfall of Metternich, the best hated man in Austria, and with him the collapse of the old régime. The Emperor Ferdinand[1] fled to Innsbruck, leaving the city in the hands of students and citizens, who formed a Committee of Public Safety. A National Diet which the Emperor had previously agreed to call met indeed, but it formed such a polyglot assembly in which a dozen different tongues and dialects strove for a hearing, that little came of its wranglings and arguments except the despatch of a deputation to Ferdinand at Innsbruck asking him to return. He did so on the 12th of August.

The Hungarians, under Kossuth, were loudly voicing their national grievances, and sent a deputation to the Diet sitting at Vienna, which it refused to receive. The Emperor resolved to appeal to arms, and appointed Bau Jellachich, a Croat, to command a very mixed force against that country. Disaffection, however, was rife in its ranks, and popular orators inflamed the people of Vienna against the undertaking. They were persuaded it was a plot which would, in the long run, tell against aspirations of their own, and it was resolved in a meeting of students and mechanics not to

---

[1] Francis had died in March, 1835. There was no music in Vienna for six weeks after.

permit any troops to leave Vienna. The railroad station was held by a detachment of the Bürger Guards, whose uniform sometimes graced the elegance of the younger Strauss. Regiments departing for Hungary were unexpectedly attacked in the streets, and a pitched battle took place on the Stefans Platz outside the Cathedral. The Bürger Guards, which held the position, were driven back into the building and overmastered there, with much slaughter. Latour, the old Minister of War, who was supposed to be responsible for a conspiracy contrary to the interests of Austria, was dragged from his office, stripped, and hanged from one of the lamp-posts in the square. The rest of the Ministers fled, and most of the members of the Diet and the richer citizens made all haste to leave the city. Ferdinand himself left Schönbrunn again on the morning of October 7th, and was escorted to Olmütz by a battalion of Hess infantry. From thence he issued a proclamation for the reduction of the city by force of arms, and Prince Windisch-Grätz was entrusted with the task. The wife of this man had been shot only a few months before while looking out of the window of her hotel in Prague, in the course of some violent rioting in that city.

The Prince took up a position at Stammersdorf and called upon the Viennese to capitulate. They were to deliver up their arms, send hostages, and hand over certain of their leaders. All clubs and journals were to be suppressed. The people rejected these demands and prepared for a desperate resistance.

The walls were heightened with sacks of earth and the gates and streets were everywhere strengthened with barricades. The fighting men in the town numbered some 25,000, and were commanded by an Austrian officer called Messenhausen. It was a small force compared with the troops and guns outside marshalled against the city, and it had no great stock of ammunition. The siege, indeed, only lasted five days. Various storming columns after a few valiant repulses succeeded in gaining possession of the suburbs and in forcing their way into the outskirts of the city.

On the 29th of October the walls were no longer tenable and an unconditional surrender followed. While the people in the evening were delivering up their arms at the appointed places, the watchmen on the top of St. Stefan's became aware that a relieving force of Hungarians was approaching. Whereupon the temper of the populace turned again. They seized their arms once more, planted their cannon on the walls, and made two spirited sallies during the battle which ensued in the country beyond. But Jellachich met the Hungarians under Kossuth and General Moya with a larger force than their own and defeated them. Then he proceeded to a fearful punitive bombardment of Vienna. On the 31st his troops forced their way into the city, and made for the Stefan's Platz where they destroyed the lamp-post upon which Latour had been hanged.

A period of violence and revenge now set in, and the city went through a terrible time. Every house was searched for revolutionaries, hundreds of prisoners were made, and thousands of people were flung into prison, or sent to serve in the Army.

Frau Strauss's apartment in the Hirschenhaus was visited by a detail of Polish soldiery. A uniform of Josef's was, however, safely hidden away, and the clever woman knew well enough how to grease the palm of a non-commissioned officer, so that the family escaped further molestation.

The Revolution ended in the abdication of the Emperor, who declared he could not cope with the times, in favour of his nephew, a boy of eighteen, Franz Josef. At the right hand of this stripling stood another Metternich, another sworn friend of privilege and autocracy, Prince Schwarzenburg.

Strauss Senior had no sympathy with the revolutionaries. He continued during all this hectic time "to feed fools with folly", i.e. to keep frivolous Vienna dancing, and reluctantly tacked some popular and topical titles to some of his pieces, titles, however, which discreetly changed with the next turn of public affairs.

Schani on the other hand got involved with the rebels. His Bürger Guard was converted into a National Guard, and he could only retain his position as Regimental Band Master by turning soldier as well. He did sentry go, in those barricaded streets of Vienna with a grandson of Goethe's, with fat Scholz and thin Nestroy. He was not by any means consumed with ardour for a patriotic death. Posted, once, in the Karmelitergasse, he heard sounds of an approaching skirmish, so promptly dumped his gun into a sentry box and dived for the neighbouring Hirschenhaus.[1] Were he required to conduct the band, however, he stood up to the work like a man. Contemporary witnesses describe him playing and conducting on the barricades, heedless of the danger and of the bullets whistling and spitting all around.

History has not, apparently, recorded anything of more interest connecting the Strausses with the Revolution than the occasion of the first production of the famous "Radetzky March".

One evening in August Johann Senior was conducting a concert on the Wasserglacis. His audience consisted of monarchists and officers, Imperial Die-Hards like himself, while the revolutionary element of workmen and students was comfortably conspicuous by its absence. The Direktor felt it a safe musical opportunity for the expression of his own political faith. After giving Beethoven's Lenore and three new waltzes of his own, came something no one had

[1] Romance has it that a melody was teasing the musician's head, and, forgetting lesser things, he rushed for pen and paper to dash down his "Revolutionsmarsch".

yet heard—a military march which fired the blood of every
soldier there. It was a stirring triumphant thing written in
honour of the conqueror of Verona. It met with a tremendous
reception and was encored three times. It was one of Strauss
senior's outstanding successes. The Radetzky March became
for the rank and file of the Austrian Army, and for every
military band throughout Europe, what Haydn's hymn
became for the Empire. This is saying a great deal, for
"the only part of Austria", writes a modern historian,[1]
"which could really claim to be a unified State filled with
a single-souled patriotism, was the Army." There was no
bullying of polyglot nationalities in the Army. When
Grillparzer hailed the great General Radetzky with:

> "Austria lies within thy camp.
> We others are mere fragments"

he assured him of the profound political truth that all of
Austria which mattered was his victorious army. The
Haydn Hymn could be no real national anthem: It was
a hymn to the Habsburgs and their vast domains. Strauss'
"Radetzky March" was the nearest (before "The Blue
Danube"), that Austria ever got to such a spiritual
possession.

It was one of the last things Strauss Vater wrote—and
one of the best things he gave his generation.

His claim indeed to remembrance may be said to found
itself upon this march and the "Lorelei Rheinklänge".
The latter work, a beautiful example of the so-called "Donau
Style" (Danube Music) was that of a true tone-poet. Schubert once remarked of the first Johann that although he
confined himself so largely to dance music, he should
certainly belong to the immortals.

In a charming little book called *Der Frühlingswalzer,*

[1] G. E. R. Gedge, *Heirs to the Habsburgs.*

G

by Robert Hohlbaum, we have the contrast between the Strausses at this period very piquantly presented. The whole sketch—for it is no more—turns on the relative positions of the two men on this particular occasion when the "Radetzky March" was first given. The star of the one is declining, that of the other is in brilliant ascent.

Strauss senior has been commissioned to write something to keep up the spirits of the old guard during this time of upheaval and distress. One evening he conducts his concert at a fashionable resort on the Glacis which is attended exclusively by his own following and that of the Emperor. In the audience sits Madame Hélène Tenora, a great actress at the Burg Theatre, dressed symbolically in *black and gold*. When Strauss electrifies the audience with his fine new "Radetzky March" he is acclaimed as perhaps never before, and at the end he does himself the honour of conducting Madame on his arm through the press of a throng for whom in her black and gold she has become the symbol of Austria herself, incarnate.

Strauss junior, on the other hand, is directing a perfectly delirious republican evening, also attended by an adoring popular actress, at a casino called the "Blaue Flasche" where he gives his *Black-red-gold* March with even more success than Strauss senior was giving his blood-stirring salute to an Imperial Field Marshal on the Wasserglacis.

Finally the two concerts are over, and the bands betake themselves home through the streets densely attended by large portions of either audience.

They encounter each other and a pitched battle ensues. Both musical and political factions fight. But the principals do not stop to see it out. They vanish—each with his particular lady—and leave matters to settle themselves in the street. Herr Hohlbaum throws them both into a mood of tenderness and regret; in the early hours of the following day Schani, leaning on the window-sill in his room, fancies he hears the strains of his father's violin on the pearly morning air. Strauss the elder, thinking of the boy that Schani had once been, has risen, and taken his bow in hand. . . .

And out of the kinder inspiration of that dawn new waltzes, of course, are born.

Schani's desertion of his post in the Karmelitergasse does not seem to have been followed by any drastic military consequences.

But it was just because he had been Band Master in the National Guard during the year of Revolution, and had written a lot of revolutionary music, that he had to wait many years after his father's death to be appointed Hoffball-musikdirektor in his turn.

CHAPTER VIII

THE elder Strauss' day was nearly over. His sun was setting.

In Heidelberg a year after the Revolution the students treated him and his orchestra with studied contempt. His great March was looked upon as a paean in triumph of the extinction of all hope of liberty for Italy . . .

He made, as we have seen, another tour, and again visited England. Here he played before Metternich. The fallen autocrat, alien and refugee, broke into tears as the strains of Vienna once more fell upon his ears.

On his return home the Master was received as usual with rapturous delight. But a curious thing happened on the 16th of September. The first time he appeared in Unger's Casino, the bow snapped in his fingers as he tucked the violin to his chin. He was feeling particularly well—made a second essay to begin—and failed. Nine days later he was dead.

One of the little daughters who had been born to him in the Andraschen House fell ill with scarlet fever. The father nursed her tenderly but collapsed in the middle of composing a new march for Radetzky. Two doctors were hastily summoned, but exhausted body and exhausted nerves offered no resistance to disease, and Strauss passed away, aged 45, at two o'clock in the morning on the 23rd of September 1849. No one knows exactly what happened immediately afterwards.

A market porter went across the canal eventually to
bring the news to the Hirschenhaus, whereupon Frau Anna
and her sons hastened at once to the dead man's abode.
On the way they passed huge placards at the street corners
announcing that the Herr Hofballmusikdirektor would
personally conduct at a banquet shortly to be given in
honour of General Radetzky. . . .

But the Hofballmusikdirektor was lying in one of the
most miserable death chambers of musical history. Left
alone in an empty apartment whence all the furniture had
been removed, the body of Johann Strauss was discovered
in a carpetless room with nothing in it but the bed. . . .
One of his sons bent over it, and gently closed the eyes.

Frau Anna looked round, but the woman about whom
she had often felt so bitterly was nowhere to be seen. Nor
was there any sign of the children.

Emilie Trampusch had disappeared.

Strauss senior left little property beyond an immense
quantity of music. What money he had went to his mistress
and her children. Johann the younger had great difficulty
later in getting from her his father's scores and instruments.
He had to buy them through some representative of the
Trampusch's. Emilie seems to have sunk into poverty.
It was discovered that she had stolen the ornamental
lanterns from her protector's grave, and pawned them to
buy food. Johann did what he could for her, but what
became of her in the end must be left to conjecture.

The news of Strauss' death, if not the manner of it,
flew through Vienna like wild fire. His loss caused an immense
sensation . . . after all he was only forty-five!

His funeral was a truly royal affair, almost as great as
Beethoven's had been in '27. Vast crowds of people lined
the route, and an important and apparently endless procession accompanied the hearse, while three bands played

alternately. Strauss was laid beside Josef Lanner in the churchyard at Döbling. The grief of the Viennese people was profound and real. It was expressed in every possible way, and was echoed in all the newspapers. Everywhere, throughout Europe, the loss was deplored, and the master was commemorated. Many years later (1905) a double momument was erected at Döblinger in memory of the two men, who had taken the folk music of the Danube waterway and translated it into terms of a world-wide appeal and beauty.

    .   .   .   .   .

It was unfortunate in some ways for Johann Strauss, the son, that his father's principal orchestra, now without a Director, should naturally look to him. Many people were only too ready to criticise the obvious step of his being asked to take it over. A decisive voice in the matter, however, was that of Strauss Vater's old first violin, that Herr Amon who had secretly taught and encouraged the son.

"Schani" gave his first concert as his father's successor ten days after Strauss' death, and shortly followed it up with a special Memorial Concert in the Sofiensaal. The programme was representative of his father's life and work from the beginning, and closed with the Radetzky March as a memorial to its own composer.

Notwithstanding this act of genuine filial piety, Strauss Junior was fiercely decried by many of those who had been sworn musical partisans of his father. He saw himself "forced into a struggle with the dead." His attitude and his actions were so cruelly misunderstood and mis-represented, that at last he was driven to defend himself and his motives in the press.

He had his widowed mother to support, he declared, and two sisters. He was far too conscious of his musical insufficiencies to wish in any way to measure himself against his father's fully acknowledged worth. Nevertheless it had become his duty five years ago at nineteen to come to the family rescue. "All the same," he wrote, "I feel my dear Father's influence is with me, it leads me to the Spirit which mourns at his grave, and urges me to show myself worthy of him."

At this date Johann's sisters, Nelli and Theresa were respectively aged twenty and eighteen. He himself was only twenty-four. One brother Josef ("Pepperl") now twenty-two, was studying architecture at the Polytechnic, and was to qualify in his profession next year. Another Edouard, at fourteen a fanatical young student of the classics, was still at school. It looks very much as if the whole family depended upon Johann.

The young man rose buoyantly to his responsibilities. He lived at home where now everything seemed completely harmonious, and worked with unsparing energy. He began writing with immense resources and fertility, and composed a whole series of those exquisitely melodious and dainty waltzes upon which his wider renown was soon to base itself.

The day was not long enough for him. When not composing, or rehearsing, he was dashing about from one place in the city to another conducting at this, that or the other festivity where he was billed "personally" to appear.

"Austrian history unrolled itself at that time as tragedy and opera bouffe in one." In the great world of affairs all sorts of horrors were taking place. The execrated Hayman (whom London draymen afterwards rolled in the mud), was at his butcher's work in Hungary, and at home, in Vienna, the young Emperor's Ministers, Bach, Brück, Kempen and Grünne were making themselves cordially

feared and hated. All hopes of a real Constitution for the
Habsburg preserves had vanished when the archiepiscopal
Palace at Kremsier where the Diet had assembled in March,
1849, was surrounded by a battalion of infantry before
daybreak and officially shut up. The only policy pursued
by the new Emperor was that of ever more and more
centralising the authority for his various domains, and that
in his person alone. There could be no patriots in Austria
but the famous "Patriots for Me". Against a dark background of oppression and reaction there was only one bright
gleam—and in its radiance the Viennese could forget the
rest.

Johann Strauss, like the Hamelin piper, drew the whole
city after him and his music.

He was no politician, he had no time to be. But musically
he could readily enough play the Vicar of Bray. The titles
of his compositions throughout the years 1848, 1849 and
1850 suffice in themselves to indicate the way things went.
It would serve little purpose here to enumerate them.
Whether or not any of this early work of Johann Strauss is
still played abroad, no echo of it, apparently, is to be heard
in England to-day. From a purely historical point of view
suffice it to mention the waltz "Freiheitslieder" (Songs of
Freedom), the "Studentenmarsch", the "Brünner National-
garde Marsch", his fifty-eighth work, this last in connection with the barricades and the Revolution, then the
"Kaiser Franz-Josef Marsch", the "Wiener Garnisons
Marsch", and a dozen more, nearing the composer's century,
identified with the all-powerful forces of reaction.

However black the times, Johann was always at hand
to lend gaiety to the superficialities of life. Never for a
moment did his fantasy or his invention fail. His mind
was a bubbling spring of melody—he said, later, his
themes were ever all about him in the Viennese air—and

write them down he must, to be rid of their delightful insistence.

However utterly weary he might be nothing stemmed the flow of his musical ideas. He is described sitting at table after a ball at the Sofiensaal, done up and exhausted. The sun is already peeping in at the windows. A member of the committee for the next rout approaches him anxiously, only just to inquire if the new waltz, promised for that very evening, is ready. The master raises his heavy head, "Not a bit of it! Haven't written a note!" but reaches for the menu, scribbles a few staves, sketches out a composition. Half an hour later, and the thing is done. This was the famous "Acceleration" waltz, written for an engineer's dance, with the amusing mechanics for its opening bars. (To-day, no doubt, Strauss could hit off an "Accelerator" waltz quite as readily.) Dozens of other charming motives just as happily occurred to a man oppressed by the morning after the night before.

Strauss had no time to sketch a thing out. He wrote the whole orchestral score at once, and gave his pages over one by one to the copyists. The same evening the composition would be played. It was often a wonder to him how a theme he had just snatched, as it were, out of the air, could please the public so mightily and meet with such rending applause.

He soon found himself at the head of a small army of first-class musicians. Every one of the numerous orchestras into which he was obliged to divide it, strode straight on from success to success, thanks to perfectly amazing training and strictest discipline. It might happen that Johann was engaged to conduct at five or more different places on the same evening. He fulfilled his contract by despatching thither his various bands, and hurrying personally from the one to the other, rendering a couple of numbers at each. "The public," says Lange, "would certainly have gone wild with indignation if they had been baulked of this glimpse of him."

He organised afternoon concerts in the Volksgarten which were so besieged that any one who could wangle a seat for himself was counted among the lucky ones. The programmes here by no means confined themselves to dance music, but were calculated to appeal to the serious musical public. Strauss conducted works which no other band-master in the city would have dared to give. "Paradoxical as it sounds," writes Lange, "Strauss, the waltz king, was the first to pave the way for Wagner in Vienna." This was quite possibly owing as much to his mother's enthusiastic appreciation of the new master, as to his own. Frau Anna Strauss and her son were perhaps the only two people in Vienna round about the eighteen-sixties who had any idea what Wagner meant. And Anna Strauss acted in some sort of a managerial capacity to her son as "Lampen-hirschl" had acted for his father. "The old Kärntnertor Theatre was fast shut against the 'dangerous Revolutionary'." The Wagner cult was regarded with high suspicion and when the enterprising Director of the Thalia Theatre in Lerchenfeld, Hoffman, produced "Tannhäuser" for the first time, he raised a host of enemies. Strauss cared nothing for all this. In giving excerpts from the Wagnerian Operas he followed the dictates of his own musical predilections. He interpreted them with his own inimitable artistry, and won for them enthusiastic applause.

The secret of his own success was that he never wrote a note which Vienna did not understand. Whether with drama, romance, or waltz, he realised it was the audience which must be captured.

Every month saw something new from his pen, apart from all the work he put in with the orchestra. Among the four hundred and seventy-nine works written by Strauss, each

of the hundred and forty-five waltzes may be divided into
five parts[1] and each part into two distinct themes, so
that it is a mere matter of arithmetic to estimate his productivity. These one thousand four hundred and fifty waltz
themes, by no means, of course, account for the whole
bulk of his work.

The history of the Strauss music is closely bound up with
the history of the dance. As the former, derived from the
Ländler, goes back to the seventeenth century and to Johann
Heinrich Schmelzer, the "Father of the Viennese School",
so the latter gradually came to transplant some very crude
peasant measures to the ballrooms of polite society. It
would take us much too far afield, here and now, even to
outline this development. As the "Volkstanz" gradually
conquered the "Baroksalon" under a succession of fiddling
and opera-writing Emperors, so it happened in our own time,
dancing became everywhere the rage. After the Napoleonic
wars people danced. They danced, high and low, after the
Great War.

They danced through the Revolution in 1848. Hence
the demand for the prolific life-work of the Strausses.

During the first twenty years of his public career Johann,
the son, wrote over three hundred dances. The second,
like the first, Johann depended upon inspiration for his
musical "ideas". But although his technical musical
education was necessarily of short duration, he was an
extremely fastidious and careful composer. Some of the
most dainty or remarkable of his passages or finales had to
be written ten, eleven or twelve times over before the
artistry of them was sufficiently cloaked by their apparent
rightness and spontaneity. It occasioned Johann an immense
amount of thought and reflection to choose between musical
alternatives. His father's work formed the foundation of

[1] A waltz of Hummel's could run into thirty-five parts.

his own, but more and more as time went on it became his endeavour to vary and enrich the forms and measures, which had determined the limits of the former's work.

It was at this point that the problem of Strauss junior began. He was not content to imitate, merely to follow, nor to leave the composition of dance music where he found it. It gradually became impossible to say anything new in the old forms. Hence he was constantly striving for new types and rhythms. A musical examination of the first twenty years of his writing brings this out in an extremely interesting way. Both Lange and Decsey devote many pages to the study and analysis of his development. It may be said, perhaps, that the bulk of Strauss' work up to the date of "Morgenblätter", 1864, belongs to the period before he fully came into his own, and to this extent has more biographical than musical interest for us to-day. But with "The Blue Danube", written in 1867, Strauss made a very significant discovery—how to relegate the three-four time of the waltz to a subordinate place, and build a bewitching melody on top of it. This was a great achievement, and drew a sharp dividing line between all his preceding and all his subsequent work.

With this one waltz, which both epitomised and crowned the first half of his life's work, Johann did for the gay and entrancing music of pleasure in Vienna, and for his own genius, what the new Emperor was presently to do for the old-time city. He broke down the inner bastions, burst its constructions, widened its prospects, and made it wholly new.

With the accession of Franz Josef the modernisation of Vienna began. The old walls and fortifications which had witnessed the Siege presently came down, the fossé and glacis were levelled, and the broad space thus created, used for the construction of the fine "Ring" boulevards of the modern city. The incorporation of the outer districts of the rapidly growing Kaiserstadt came with the destruction of the outer ramparts, or Linien Graben, in 1890. It is with this later Vienna, the city soon to be queened by one of the most beautiful wayward and tragic Empresses the world has ever seen, that the greater part of the younger Johann Strauss' life is to be identified, and in which it ran its superficial and brilliant course. His "Demolition Polka", for instance, was written in 1862 to mark the throwing down of the old walls and bastions.

In spite of plenty of the adverse criticism which every ambitious or successful artist naturally incurs, Johann attained a giddy height of popularity by the year 1850. His Sunday afternoon concerts in the Volksgarten attracted all the "best people". No dance or ball of any consequence was given without him. There were for the new-comer only three sights in Vienna, the Kärntnertor Theatre, St. Stefan and Johann Strauss. The famous Direktor now began to figure largely in the press, and everywhere the caricaturists busied themselves with so spirited and handsome a subject. A lithograph of Kriehuber in 1855 shows him as yet without the amazing Dundreary whiskers which, later, formed the *beau idéal* of manly beauty. Strauss made a striking picture right up to the end, but as a young man of thirty there was still more of the poet about him than of what has amusingly been called "the cat on the tiles". He had a well-formed head, with a broad, high brow, from which the shining black hair swept back to a mass of glossy curls. The dark vivacious eyes were set well apart under firmly marked brows. The nose was well modelled, and at this date a flowing moustache and touch of beard under the lower lip did nothing to hide a good mouth and pleasing line of chin and jaw. A head like this rose above a turn-down collar with flowing artistic tie, and studded shirt-front gleaming

between the immense reveres of the sort of frock-coat affected
by the dandies of the period.

Johann was the darling of Vienna and ranked second in
importance only to the young Emperor himself. At a
musical competition held in the Sperl in 1852 a waltz of
his, the "Johanniskaferln", carried the day, even when
pitted against a number by the famous gypsy composer,
Kalozdy.

Strauss was obliged, much against his will, to make a
foreign tour in 1851, and after immense successes at Prague,
Dresden and Leipzig, he attempted to proceed via Breslau
to Warsaw. But he had no pass, and was held up
for two hours at the Russian frontier, together with his
orchestra, by an unenlightened individual who had never
even heard of him. The whole suspicious-looking company
would have been clapped in irons and forwarded without
ceremony to Siberia, but for the timely arrival of a messenger
from no less a personage than the Czarina. Whereupon
Authority, astonished and relieved, but still growling, observed, "Well, supposing you *had* been bandits, you or I
would have been sent into exile, and I'd rather you than me."

Johann was rapturously received on his return home.
Vienna could not now get on without him. There were
at least eight resorts of the élite which despaired in the
absence of their idol, the Diana Bad, the Schwenderi,
the Neue Welt, Volksgarten, Blumensale and Sofiensale,
the Viktoria Hotel and Dommayer's, to say nothing of the
Sperl. The finest of all these palaces of pleasure, the
Odeonsaal in the Leopoldstadt, had been burnt in the black
months of revenge following the Revolution. Not only
could the Viennese not live without Johann, it even seemed
they could not die without him. One worthy lady
made the stipulation in her will that Strauss should be
played at her funeral—which indeed he was. This may

possibly be the only recorded occasion when a waltz served as a dirge.

No nervous system could stand the strain indefinitely. Johann was near to breaking down, and his doctors urgently advised him to take a rest. The all-important question was who should carry on in his absence? Neither the orchestra nor its "Manager", Frau Strauss, had far to look for an understudy. The genius of the family had not confined itself to one member. One and all they pitched upon Josef to understudy Johann.

Josef, two years his brother's junior, was the nineteenth-century pacifist of the family. His father had wanted him to become a soldier. But during the Revolution he wrote "I do not wish to learn how to kill men. I do not wish to win distinction by hunting down my kind. Better to seek death at once than go about with such a conscience. Let me be where I am. Let me be what I am."

He was a singularly gifted young man, but instead of choosing music, literature or painting as a career, he had become an architectural draughtsman, and had put in some time as engineer in a spinning factory. He was now deep in his work, and full of plans for prosecuting further studies when, all of a sudden like a bolt from the blue, Johann pounced on him to take over the orchestra.

The two brothers were very unlike, the one vivacious, gay and dandified, the other monkish in appearance and disposition. It went tremendously against the grain of Josef to be suddenly and unexpectedly called upon to fill a position of which he had never dreamed, and for which he was far too modest to feel that his own musical attainments would suffice. He did his utmost, but in vain, to refuse, and so embarked upon a quite unforeseen career, which he was nevertheless to pursue henceforth with enthusiasm and success.

"Dearest Linchen," he wrote to his fiancée, "the unavoidable has happened. . . . I am frightfully sorry about it, but comfort myself with the hope (at my first appearance) that you will be thinking of me, as I of you."

He took over the Master's orchestra, which, unlike Johann, he conducted with a baton instead of the bow, and the latter retired for a well-earned rest first to Gastein and then to Bad Neuhaus, accompanied by his mother's sister, Tante Weber.

CHAPTER IX

WHILE he was on holiday Strauss met some important Russian railway magnates, who seem to have been possessed with a flair for advertising. They were extremely anxious to promote traffic over their lines, and conceived the brilliant idea of inviting the famous Viennese Director to inaugurate a series of concerts during the next few summer seasons—from May to the end of September—at Pavlovsk near St. Petersburg. They would put the newly built and princely "Vauxhall" at his disposal. In addition they offered him a magnificent salary, free transportation, service and apartments. This offer was made in 1854, the year of the young Emperor's marriage to Princess Elizabeth of the royal House of Bavaria.

All Vienna had taken part in the brilliant ceremonies and festivities of that April. The sixteen-year-old bride had travelled down the Danubian waterway smothered in flowers. She was received by the enthusiastic Austrian people first at the frontier, and then at Nussdorf at the portals of the Kaiserstadt. They accompanied her in triumphant procession overnight to Schönbrunn, and next day saw her even more magnificent entry to Vienna for her marriage. The city was packed with visitors of the utmost distinction, and with crowds and crowds of sightseers. Everywhere flowers, garlands, decorations, illuminations, festivities and music and dancing were the order of the day. Elizabeth came riding in a golden coach drawn by eight milk-white horses, a veritable fairy princess of youth and loveliness. She was in pink silk embroidered all over with silver, and crowned with a diadem of diamonds entwined with white and red roses. She and the youthful Franz Josef contracted that marriage, which was to be one long strange tragedy, in the Augustinian Church near the Hofburg and the same night, of course, there was a great court ball.

In the Zeremoniensaal der k.k. Hofburg, 27 April, 1854 Strauss conducted the beautiful "Myrtlekränze" (Crown of Myrtle, Bride's Wreath) waltz which he had specially written for these days of Imperial festivity.

Meanwhile he had accepted the Russian offer, and next year he proceeded to St. Petersburg with an entirely new orchestra (leaving Josef to look after his musical interests in Vienna), where the most optimistic anticipations of the Railway Company were abundantly justified. High Russian Society took Strauss to its heart. He became as much the rage at Pavlovsk and at St. Petersburg as he was at home. People flocked to his concerts from far and near. The Grand Duke Constantine, a brother of the Emperor, was so overwhelmed with admiration for the Austrian wizard that he begged to be allowed to play the 'cello with him!

Evening after evening Strauss was carried home shoulder high by the enthusiastic Russians. He could only escape the crowds awaiting him after a concert by slipping away from the hall by some exit at the back, more or less in disguise. He had all sorts of fantastic adventures. The women, of course, "fell" for him right and left.

Glorious publicity pushed to great extremes enabled Strauss to put in twelve seasons at the Russian capital. His polkas delighted the public even more than his waltzes. He wrote some charming music especially for this public, among other numbers the Fantasy for the piano called "In a Russian Village", and the polkas "L'Inconnue" and "Olga". Later he composed a "Coronation March" for the Imperial Russian pair, Alexander II and Maria Alexandrovna, on the occasion of their accession in 1857.

The inflated salaries he received during these seasons laid the foundations of his fortune. He always returned to Vienna tremendously in funds; and thanks to the aunt, his mother's sister, Frau Josephine Weber, who accompanied him to St. Petersburg, he was prevented from spending there as thoughtlessly and as lavishly as he might otherwise have done. Back home again his mother seems to have kept a sharp eye on his finances, and to have saved his money for him. She produced it, in bulk, on a certain day in August, 1862.

Johann had contrived to reach his thirty-seventh year without capitulating in marriage to any one among the countless host of his fair admirers. He was, secretly or professedly, the cynosure of all their bright eyes, the prince of their dreams, the prize of their most jealous ambitions. Very possibly the Waltz King of Vienna could have picked up a wife from the richest set in society, if not from that final and rigidly exclusive sphere at the very top. He belonged, really, to all the fair of Vienna. Not one of them but had a glimmer—or perhaps a real flicker—of hope. Sighs and ardours encircled him . . . every sort of adoration was laid at his feet.

He is supposed to have had a more or less ill-defined love affair with a girl called Reserl Wohlgemut, that daughter of a neighbour in the Hirschenhaus to whom he gave piano lessons as a boy, in order to earn a little money for the secret pursuit of his own musical education. The story has formed the basis of a screen play abroad. Reserl despaired at last of her wayward bedazzled "Jean," and married some one else not long before his own matrimonial fate was sealed. Johann was for years the recipient of endless feminine

letters, from high and low alike, couched in every form of
lovesick "Schwärmerei". We can imagine him impatient
over an accumulation of them, while a brother or sister,
marvelling, laughing, and just a trifle curious, opens a few
at random and reads them aloud for the fun of the thing.
Screen stars of the present day, afflicted or flattered in the
same nonsensical way, would sympathise with this idol of
the past.

All of a sudden the thunderbolt fell, and Viennese female
society was thrown into hysterics. Johann had made his
choice, an astonishing, incredible choice. It left everybody
thunderstruck, gaping, and broke innumerable foolish hearts.
It was a first-class society sensation—and it loosened tongues
wherever malice, disappointment, envy, curiosity and all the
other less creditable passions of the human heart found vent
in gossip and scandalmongering. A few there may have
been, especially among men like Johann's old friend and
publisher, Haslinger, who understood and who dared pre-
dict success.

But even Haslinger had known nothing of it beforehand.
One day towards the end of August, 1862, a note was put
into his hand from Strauss. It begged him in a jocular line
or two to act as best man at his—Johann's—wedding at
seven o'clock next morning in St. Stefan's.

The bride to be was Henrietta Treffz!

Henrietta Treffz! Of all people. . . !

Charming, yes. Still beautiful and vastly attractive, but
years older than the bridegroom, and a very, very, "experienced" lady. An artist, too, almost as fine a singer as Jenny
Lind, and equally beloved—years ago—of the public. But
with two sorts of a past, a remote one, and a proximate
one as the long-established mistress of Baron Todesco, a
Jewish financier and the mother of his daughter!

How on earth, asked everyone, had this thing come about?

By courtesy of the Director of the Historical Collections of the City of Vienna.

JOHANN STRAUSS, SOHN.

The lady whom society had tacitly agreed to accept without expressly acknowledging her, had been the head of an important household in Vienna since her retirement from the operatic stage some years before.

It was at a ball given at Baron Todesco's at which Johann Strauss had been specially invited by this lady to conduct the music, that he and she fell violently in love. They were both highly temperamental people. Both were accomplished musicians, and so the two inflammable natures simply caught fire from each other.

Once this happened, cost what it might, nothing was allowed to stand in their way. The Treffz, apparently, made short work of her entanglement with the Baron, and Johann, for his part, swept aside every hindrance or other consideration. This thing was serious. They made no great fuss about their wedding, but betook themselves early that August morning to Church, in ordinary dress, accompanied by none but a few confidential friends. After that Vienna could make what it liked of the *fait accompli*.

They went first to an apartment in the Weihburggasse, but this has long since given place to newer buildings. A few years later they moved to the Praterstrasse in the Leopoldstadt, to a house with a charming garden attached, where "The Blue Danube" came to be written. In 1870 they acquired a house in Hietzing, where they settled down very happily.

In marrying Henrietta Treffz and establishing himself with her in very considerable style, Johann Strauss was making quite a fresh departure. He had reached a new turning point in a career already highly successful. From now on he became a no less popular but a far more imposing person. His wife, an accomplished woman of the world, possessed an unbounded admiration for Strauss's gifts and achievements, and a fine talent for advancing his career.

She devoted herself to him and it, and supplied energy at all points where any suggestion in him of Viennese inertia might have militated against it. Metaphorically speaking, she took this home-loving Austrian by the scruff of his neck, dumped him on board trains and ships, and steered him from one triumph to another half round the world.

This is, however, to anticipate a little. Strauss's first wife deserves a biographical paragraph or so to herself.

She came, we are told, of good middle-class Viennese folk. Her father was a silversmith in Gumpendorf, and her mother married a solicitor of the name of Treffz. "Jetty" seems to have been left much to her own devices. She went on the stage early and grew up in the theatre where she soon achieved success.

She appeared in the Kärntnertor Theatre in 1837 and made a distinct hit with Auber's "Sirène". A glowing future was forecast for her, and later on the "Bohemian Napoleon", Pockorny, cast her with some contemporary notabilities for an opera of his own. Vienna was raving at that time over Jenny Lind, but Berlioz in his letters could still find praises for the Treffz. Her star was in the ascendant. She went on tour in Germany, spent the Revolution year in England, and returned to Vienna full of triumphs, determined gracefully to retire. No one knows exactly what age she may have been then, but she was doubtless well capable of gaining for herself whatever good things in life she desired. Possibly these were embodied for her in the Baron Todesco.

When, therefore, she suddenly left him for a man perhaps ten years her junior, and, to the momentary indignation of all feminine Vienna, carried off the idol of the city, Jetty Treffz meant that Johann was whisked right out of the Hirschenhaus, into far more socially pretentious surroundings, and a still more ambitious professional sphere.

She had taste, as taste went in Vienna in the eighteen-

fifties and sixties, and furnished their house suitably for the
newly appointed Director of Dance Music to the Court
(1864).[1]

Throughout all this time the face of Vienna was changing.
Originally—that is to say from the date when success first
came to him up to the moment of his marriage—Johann
was busy enough playing night after night in the various
resorts of the city, on Monday at Dommayer's, Tuesday in
the Volksgarten, Wednesday at the "Grüner Zeisig",
Thursday at the "Blaue Flasche" in Lerchenfeld, Friday
at the English Restaurant in Währing, Saturday at the
Sperl, and on Sunday at Unger's Casino in Hernals.

Fashionable and aristocratic Vienna frequented the Volksgarten, and the audiences here were also composed of people
from the circles of high finance and from the intelligentsia
of the University. At "Papa" Dommayer's were to be seen
prosperous manufacturers and business men, most of them
rolling in money. The Zeisig and the English Restaurant
attracted the smaller tradesmen and operatives who sought
recreation of an evening. While the Sperl remained an ever-
popular rendezvous for the gay ladies of the Viennese pave-
ments, and was always a good place for assignations, the
"Blaue Flasche" in Lerchenfeld frankly catered for those
who rejoiced in lack of morals as well as culture, and who
would have pawned their last rag for a drink and a dance at
Valentin's.

But with the constant modernisation and extension of
Vienna, and the inclusion of its ever-growing suburbs, many
of these localities began to look old-fashioned with their
rather fusty furnishings and poor illumination. A gigantic
new dance hall was provided by the roofing in of the Sofien-
bad, and still further out, near the gates of Schönbrunn

[1] Strauss held this appointment until 1870 when he and Jetty moved
to Hietzing.

itself a vast building called the Kolosseum was opened for the same purpose. The smart dances (Élitebälle) given in the former, and the masquerades in the latter, provided the pleasure-loving city with fresh sensations.

And everywhere Strauss was in command. Vienna was, of course, possessed of a perfect legion of orchestras civil and military, many of them directed by musicians, like Waldteufel, well up to the mark of Strauss himself, but for all that it was Johann who was in most clamorous request. Whenever a great public body, like the lawyers' corporation or the doctors', or the engineers', decided to give a big public ball, the Committee not only approached Strauss first, but refused to proceed without him. Many of his pieces were specially written for these occasions as their amusing titles sufficiently indicate. For the lawyers he wrote the "Juristenballtänze" (The Jurists dance), the "Solonsprüche" (Judgments of Solomon), the "Kontroversen" (Arguments); for the doctors, "Panaceaklänge" (Panacea chords), "Leberswecker" (Liver shaker), "Erhöte Pulse" (heightened pulse); for the technicians, "Schallwellen" (Sound waves), "Sirenen" (Sirens), "Schwungräder" (Flywheels), "Akzelerationen" (Acceleration), and a dozen more.

Nor was Strauss heedless of the armies of men employed in the transformation of the ancient city, levelling the walls, filling up the moats, laying out magnificent new boulevards. He wrote the "Demolierer Polka" for them, a sort of Board-of-Works note in music! Nothing in bureaucratic Habsburg Vienna was more truly democratic than the bow and fiddle of this wizard.

At length Vienna took on the appearance of a vast and beautiful modern metropolis, and the style of living of all classes, particularly the rich, rose in keeping with it. The nobility was now housed in vast palaces, however strictly

it still kept to itself, and the famous Prater offered a bewildering spectacle of prosperity and glitter, especially on the
Monday in Easter Week, when all the rank of beauty and
fashion of the city turned out to go driving in the sunshine,
to the gaping admiration of the bourgeoisie.

The woman who became Strauss's wife had moved by
virtue of her position in Baron Todesco's house, in that
"aristocracy of finance" in Vienna which rose there after
1815. It was these families, coming for the most part from
the trade and industrial centres of southern Germany, who
opened their salons to the artists and musicians of the
previous period. They had begun to help in the constitution
of an educated public opinion, even in matters outside the
arts. It was very advantageous to Strauss, now, to have the
Treffz's experience and influence turned wholly to account
for the benefit of his career. Up to this time he had occasionally deputised for the Director of the Court Dance Music,
but not yet had his activities in 1848 been officially forgiven
him. It had been long, indeed, before the Strauss waltzes
were allowed at court at all, although the Emperor himself
privately delighted in them. At length, however, he was
appointed to the position his father had held before him,
and he became one of the few people in Vienna who could
pass easily from one of its social water-tight compartments
to the other.

" Viennese court society was still, in essentials, very much
what it had been under Maria Theresa and Joseph II,
purely aristocratic and utterly exclusive. Outside this was
ranged the "Second Society" consisting of old but newly
ennobled families of officials, generals and great merchants
and industrialists. Then came a third circle, the productive
middle-class, which established contact with the two
preceding through a fourth, the bankers and financiers.
Vienna's professional men were somewhat isolated. The

physicians, lawyers, writers and her leaders in technical and industrial advance, were cut off by this rigid tripartite constitution of society from all contact with the Court."[1] But the middle class was growing up throughout these decades, and was developing rapidly, and making contacts in all possible directions.

Strauss appealed to all classes of society in Vienna, from the lowest to the highest. In the year of his marriage he mounted the topmost rung of his own social ladder. In so doing he struck, as it were, a chord of harmony throughout the city, and established at least one plane upon which its citizens delighted to stand in common.

From this time on Strauss was obliged by sheer pressure of work largely to retire from the conductor's desk in most of his accustomed concert halls, particularly in the Vorstadt, appearing only on special occasions, or on the first nights of his latest compositions. He gave his orchestras over to the direction of his brothers, for now Edouard also had been irresistibly drawn to music in his wake, and by dint of hard and serious study both were acquiring reputations as executants and as writers second only to his own.

He went off to Russia again, taking his wife with him, where she made a brilliant "last" appearance at one of the concerts at court, and he devoted himself to writing a whole series of works specially in her honour.

[1] *" Emperor Francis Joseph of Austria."*   Redlich.

CHAPTER X

THE STORY OF "THE BLUE DANUBE", '66–'67

IT is interesting to note that Johann Strauss senior began the custom of giving titles to his compositions. It was so much simpler to refer to the "Kettenbrücke Walzer" i.e. the waltz written for the Gasthaus at Kettenbrücke, instead of to the *Opus* number. When the sum of the dances began to mount up—and Johann Strauss junior wrote about three hundred and fifty between 1844 and 1872—it became far more handy to name them distinctively rather than by their number in the series.

Behind every one of these prolific melodies there is a story. Each Strauss Waltz was written under circumstances of individual interest, and produced at a special place, or for a particular occasion. Many of them were dedicated to the distinguished notabilities of the day. The "Morgenblätter" (Morning Papers) for instance was composed in direct competition with Offenbach's "Die Abendblätter", when the famous Parisian visited Vienna in 1864. Johann had not been anxious to accept this invitation from a ball committee to pit his wits against those of so formidable a rival. In spite of all his success and popularity, he yet retained a very saving sense of his own limitations, and was at heart a modest artist. Offenbach, indeed, triumphed on this particular occasion by public acclaim, but the fact still remains that whereas "Die Abendblätter" soon came to be forgotten, "Die Morgenblätter" long survived.

Fritz Lange has a very good answer for those critics who accused Strauss of hastiness or carelessness in composition. "On the one hand," he said, "people belauded his inexhaustible fertility of invention, and on the other found fault with his failure fully to develop his themes." They put this down to his "Austrian superficiality", and to the hasty sketchiness of conception resulting from it. That many of the Strauss dances exhibit indications of a certain nervous haste in composition, cannot be denied. How could this be otherwise, considering how incessant and clamorous was the demand for the popular master's work? He was forever being plagued for new dances. The work of a man who never had a quiet moment, who lived for ever in full evening dress, whose bow was never out of his hand except when the pen was in it, ought not to be judged in cold blood by the highest canons of musical taste.

Once, however, when owing to marriage and his appointment as Director of Dance Music at Court, Strauss found himself thoroughly well established, he was freed to a great extent from the driving necessity of composition and personal rush-about. He began to write a series of choice waltzes. "The Beautiful Blue Danube", which deserves a chapter to itself, was the greatest of them all.

Meantime the Director was getting tired of his publisher, Edouard Haslinger, successor to Beethoven's Haslinger. and himself a composer, seems to have treated Johann much after the accepted manner of Viennese music publishers. They got on fairly well together, arrant exploitations notwithstanding, and Johann delivered himself of many a joke and sarcasm at the other's expense, as when on one occasion Haslinger wrote "heart-felt and sincere greetings to Frau Strauss" and the composer retorted that his correspondent, as publisher, did not know the meaning of the second adjective. At last, however, there was no fun left in the situation, and Johann made other arrangements. He concluded a contract with the publisher Spina, whereby in consideration of an annual retaining fee he was to write six dances every year. He wrote, of course, many more than this, but the agreement held until 1874, when he gave up the composition of individual dance numbers.

Like every prolific writer ever on the look-out for good titles, Strauss kept a list of suggestive names and lines which he and his publisher now and again passed in careful review. Among others he had noted down the last line of a verse written by quite a negligible poet, Karl Beck, who, had he never written anything else, hereby achieved vicarious immortality.

"Und ich sah dich reich an Schmerzen,
Und ich sah dich jung und hold,
Wo die Treue wächst im Herzen
Wie im Schacht das edle Gold,
An der Donau, *an der schönen blauen Donau*."

"And I saw you in all your trouble,
And I saw you young and sweet,
Where fidelity grows in the heart,
Like gold found in the mine,
On the Danube, the beautiful blue Danube."

It was the line "an der schönen blauen Donau" which struck the composer. Complete townsman as he was, living the most artificial life possible, Johann Strauss yet loved the country, the Viennese woods, hills, and river, the Danube, as the purest and richest source of all his melodic inspiration.

When as now for the first time he had to write a waltz for a song Beck's line suggested itself to his mind, by way of a title. He did not want the verse.

Vienna was just recovering from the anxieties and defeats and heavy losses of the Austro-Prussian War, one of the shortest and most decisive campaigns of modern times, which broke out in 1866.

Austria had no chance against the forces of William I and Bismarck. Her armies only took the field as someone once said, "to make the reputations of opposing generals."

The horrors of the disaster for the inhabitants of the Kaiserstadt were somewhat similar, on a very much smaller scale, to the horrors suffered in London during the Great War. At least the letters written by people in Vienna at that time give this impression. Troop trains brought terrible loads of wounded back to the city after the slaughter one fierce July day at Königgratz, (Sadowa). There were 200,000 men engaged on either side. The scenes at the station were comparable to those at Victoria in our own times, except that the reception and relief organisation was not so efficient or so neatly uniformed. We read of chocolate and tobacco for the soldiers, and of hysterical women rushing about and getting in the way of those who kept their heads.

There had been ardent pacifists in Berlin, like the Empress Augusta who flung herself at the Emperor's feet in tears to implore him to stave off this thing, and like the famous Austrian Baroness von Suttner whose book, " *Lay down your Arms* ", has become a classic of Peace propaganda—people to whom the spectacle of Austrian militarism in Italy wrought only anguish and a noble indignation. But they could make no headway against the War Lords of their day, so there was an interlude of bombast and butchery, and a temporary eclipse of gaiety in Vienna. The war, however, only lasted seven weeks. The Austrian forces were very inferior in equipment and in leadership to the Prussian. After Sadowa, King William intended to march on to Vienna and compel her to pay a heavy indemnity, and to concede part of her territory to Prussia. His troops neared the city. Floridsdorf indeed, to the north, was in imminent danger of attack.

But Bismarck threatened to resign if Austria were to be too deeply humiliated. An end had been put to her influence upon German politics. So she was allowed to patch up a losing deal with Italy, and to conclude the Peace of Prague with Prussia, after which the order of the day, as far as Strauss was concerned, was "As you were".

The most important of the Men's Choral Societies in Vienna meeting again for the first time after this deluge of blood and iron, commissioned the most famous Kapelle-meister in the city to write something very special for the occasion.

Johann Strauss's "Beautiful Blue Danube" was the gesture he made. Whereupon the Kaiserstadt rapidly recovered its volatile spirits and began to sing and dance again.

It was Johann Herbeck, the Director of the Viennese Male Choral Society, who induced Strauss to write for the voice. The two men greatly admired each other. Herbeck was in need of a good song for his choir, and thought Strauss just the man to produce one. Johann, however, strongly rebutted the suggestion. He said he knew nothing of song-writing and that in any case a hundred voices would be too many for any song. Herbeck persisted, saying that one of the elder Johann's waltzes had been quite successfully adapted for the voice. His friend waved this aside. He was afraid, he insisted, of running the risk of boring the public, or of exhausting his own invention; whereat Herbeck laughed immoderately, and reminded the other of Schumann's saying that to be prolific is characteristic of genius.

It was quite in keeping with the queer admixture of musical daring and personal diffidence in Johann that he

allowed himself to be persuaded at length to attempt this
new thing. And it was also in keeping with much else in
his musical history that the outstanding achievement of his
life, his greatest, his immortal waltz, should at first be
shackled by a jingling rhyme, and should meet with no
marked initial success. For Herbeck carried his point, leaving
Johann committed to the composition of a choral waltz.

Sitting in his study on the first floor of the house in the
Praterstrasse, Johann bethought himself of the paternal
"Rheinklänge", and composed his own tone poem on the
Danube—his "Symphony in Blue" as it has been called.
It was the spirit not of the actual river he designed to
translate into music, but of the Austrian feeling for that long
majestic water highway. Unlike so many descriptive
passages in Strauss which echo the sounds of nature, the
flutings of birds, the silvery plash of waters, the deep bass
of the wind in the tree tops, or whichever reproduce the whirr
and hum of machinery, "The Blue Danube" transmutes
rather than paints. It is no realistic picture of the river,
but rather a melody enshrining its soul. It was he, not
Karl Beck, who discovered the Danube for Vienna, who
elevated the geographical consciousness of the city to heights
of charming poesy. Strauss even invested the great stream
with its eternal blue, since in reality it is only when the
heavens are in smiling mood that its greenish waters are so
transformed. The Danube *can* be blue. Looking upstream
towards Klosterneuberg from the Stephaniewarts, a watch
tower upon a wooded height above the city, on a fine sunny
day, it can be all the waltz suggests. Otherwise it is dis-
appointing in this respect. Franz Léhar, indeed, composed
a Lamentations Waltz in 1919 called "The Grey Danube,"
in which the Strauss motives "undergo a sad loss of colour."
It would seem a new tone-poem is required to-day, again,
to bring the Danube musically up to date!

The German biographers of Strauss have written pages of learned analysis, both musical and metaphysical, of his more important works, and of " The Blue Danube " in particular, in an attempt to answer the question wherein exactly lies its peculiar charm.

It would be beyond the pretensions of the present book to do more than record the fact that the Strauss music has been accorded this serious and expert study. The beauty of this waltz, for instance, is held to consist in its simplicity, in a "Simplicity which was at the same time one of the most lovely and daring ventures in musical art. This experiment consisted in deriving thirty-two measures of melodious intoxication from a single key, in drawing so much from a single motive, a triad in D major ".

The reader who would like to pursue this study could not do better than read the masterly pages written on " The Blue Danube " alone by authorities like Lange and Decsey.

More than one attempt was made to write suitable words for the new composition. But Strauss crossed them all out. Nothing seemed happy enough. Nothing exactly suited. As a matter of fact, words came to be written for " The Blue Danube " over and over again, both in German and French, but nothing ever succeeded for the reason that the music was self-sufficient, and had no need of them. For the moment the Choral Society's own poet, Josef Weyl—an official of Viennese Police—supplied a jingle which served:

"Wiener seid froh!
Oho, wieso?
Ein schimmer des Lichts,
Wir sehen noch nichts." [1]

[1] "Be gay, Viennese!
Oh ho, why so?
A shimmer of light,
But for us it's still night."

I

The new work, for which Strauss's publisher (Spina) only gave him a hundred and fifty gulden [1]—was performed on the evening of the 15th of February, 1867, in the Dianasaal by the famous orchestra of the brothers Josef and Edouard, assisted by the Viennese Male Voice Choir.

It was received with warm appreciation, but not more. It has even been said that at first "The Blue Danube" was a failure. This can scarcely be so, since it aroused the usual Strauss applause and was encored.

Six months were to go by, however, before the piece truly came into its own.

At the instance of a Frenchman, the Comte D'Osmond, an enthusiastic frequenter of the Strauss concerts in the Imperial Volksgarten in Vienna, the Direktor was invited to attend the great International Exhibition being held in Paris in the summer of 1867.

A good many difficulties, it seems, had to be surmounted before he could accept. Only when a suitable orchestra and a suitable concert hall were assured to him did he consent.

To gain any idea of what an amazing thing this Exhibition was, of how brilliant a season attended it, the reader should be thoroughly versed in the chronicles of the Second Empire—not the political chronicles, nor any chronicles more important than those of society and the boulevards, of Figaro, of the theatre, of French operetta, of the gay life, and of scandal—for the "glamour and joy" which were supposed to have descended incarnate upon Paris (and the rest of the earth) when Napoleon and Eugénie were married, ruled triumphantly now, and had succeeded in thrusting everything of the slightest real importance in life not only into the background but utterly out of sight.

---

[1] A gulden was worth, at that time, about two shillings, so Strauss received about £15 for the most famous waltz he ever wrote.

The Empress was queening it at the Tuileries, very much with the help of the Princess Metternich; Hortense Schneider in the title rôle of Offenbach's immense Exhibition success "The Grand Duchess of Gerolstein" was drawing all the titled heads of Europe to the court of her dressing-room at the Variétés; that amazing figure of nineteenth-century journalism, and publicity Villemessant, was at the height of his power; and a perfect firmament of stars in all the gayer walks of life flashed and sparkled in the Fields Elysian.

Paris was in a delirium of gaiety. Society never went to bed. All the theatres were in full swing, and night after night routs and balls and concerts all over the city kept the festivities at fever height.

The Exhibition, the most ambitious assemblage of products, pavilions, incongruities, novelties, the world has seen up to that time, not excepting the Crystal Palace, served more as a lodestone to Paris than as a stimulus to trade or education, or as a glorification of the French, or whatever purpose of this sort it may ever have proposed to itself. The Exhibition grounds were surrounded by pleasure resorts of every description. It was a sort of world's fête.

Plunging into such a vortex as this even Johann Strauss at first went under!

He was lost. No one heard of him. His concerts failed to make a hit.

It was very soon apparent that even a reputation such as that of the Waltz King of Vienna was not enough in itself to ensure attention in Paris during Exhibition time.

He was billed, to be sure, as follows, at one of the concert halls and restaurants immediately in the vicinity of the Exhibition.

CERCLÉ INTERNATIONALE

CONCERT PROMENADE

À L'INSTAR DES CONCERTS PROMENADES DE LONDRES
ET DE VIENNE

DONNÉ PAR
JOHANN STRAUSS
Chef de musique des bals de la cour impérial et royal D'Autriche

ET
B. BILSE
Musikdirektor de sa Majesté le Roi de Prusse

But the announcement made no particular stir.

By way of a glance at one of the festivities in Paris at this time we have only to turn up the faded pages of the *London Illustrated News*, for the pictures, or read the letters of the Paris correspondent to the *Daily Telegraph*. This gentleman writes on one occasion: "It is by no means easy to entertain —and I mean that in both senses of the word—two thousand persons, including an Emperor, an Empress, an Imperial Prince, a King, two Queens, two royal Princes, Grand Duchesses, Highnesses, and all the diplomacy, wit, beauty and fashion of a great city; yet that was what was not only attempted but thoroughly effected on Friday. . . . The gate of a great Hotel wide open, and guarded jealously by the inevitable picket of police—a court illuminated by great glittering gas stars . . . the stream of carriages began to flow at nine and went on till twelve. . . ." All the familiar features of the approach to this Hotel had "disappeared with the garden itself, and in their place was fairyland. At the end a trellis covered with ivy and creepers of every kind: in the centre a bed of flowers and a glittering fountain;

on either side galleries lined with flowers; and above a splendid light without which no ball is possible; add to this a group of the best-looking and best-dressed people in Paris and you may have a faint idea of the beauty of a scene which astonished the eyes of those who have been ball-going ever since they could run alone."

This was the sort of festivity to which Paris was giving itself up, all through those wonderful summer months in 1867. Strauss at the Cercle Internationale was comparatively lost. He needed a good publicity agent.

The first to come forward in this capacity was no less brilliant and bewildering a personage than the one woman in Paris only less important than the Empress Eugénie herself—the brightest jewel indeed in the very flashing crown worn by society in the Exhibition year—the Princess Pauline Metternich, wife of the Austrian Ambassador to the Court of Napoleon III.

It was this amazing woman, this "belle laide" as she was called, at once *grande dame*, at home in the most rigidly exclusive circles of the Viennese aristocracy, and—abroad—emancipated eccentric given to smoking immense cigars, who assisted the Empress Eugénie to transform a bourgeoise Paris into the Ville Lumière beloved of the whole gay world. Memoirs of the time abound in anecdotes, many of them daring to the point of scandal, about the arresting and often irresponsible actions and undertakings of the fascinating Austrian. She was an outstanding figure at the French Court during the Second Empire, and was the cynosure of the whole of society's envious, admiring eyes.

The English correspondents' letters were full of her, as they are full of accounts of the most gorgeous balls and routs and daring costumes. "The Austrian Ambassadress was, I think, *the* flower of the parterre. Sèvres china, started into life . . . is the only idea I can give you of the *belle bergère* who . . . accompanied the Emperor through the whole suite of rooms.

"The Austrian Embassy has commenced its weekly receptions. It is neutral ground: everybody meets everybody, and the result is agreeable. The Metternich princesses are always witty. . . .

"Look at the Empress, Princess Metternich, . . . they are dressed to perfection . . . otherwise I am never weary of watching the vagaries of Paris fashion. 'Une robe qui commence à peine et finit tout de suite' describes the fashionable mode. Add to this development the very shortest of waists, the longest of trains, and you have the picture of the best-dressed woman in Paris."

It was the Princess Metternich who took Strauss up and decided to patronise her distinguished compatriot. She arranged a sumptuous ball at the Austrian Embassy at which he should conduct the music.

Everywhere, of course, at the Embassy, were massed banks of flowers, artificial cascades, multicoloured illuminations, galaxies of flashing scintillating candelabra fringed and encrusted with rainbow lustres. There were lackeys and police, duchesses and diamonds, peers and orders, and uniforms of every describable and indescribable gorgeousness. All this to introduce Monsieur Strauss in person. . . .

An American lady who was present at the Princess's ball (Madame de Hegermann Lindencrone) afterwards wrote of it in a letter (Paris, May 29th, 1867):

"No one thought of dancing: everyone wanted to listen to his (Strauss') waltz. And how Strauss played it! . . . With what fire and entrain! We had thought Waldteufel perfect but when you had heard Strauss you said to yourself you had never heard a waltz before.

"The musicians were partly hidden by gigantic palmetios, plants and pots of flowers arranged in the most attractive way. But he—Johann Strauss—stood well in the front looking very handsome, very Austrian, and very pleased with himself. . . . The music was inspiring enough to have made an Egyptian mummy get out of his sarcophagus and caper. . . . The cotillon finished at half-past five in the morning."

Marvellous as the evening was, it still fell short of complete recognition for Strauss. He was not yet "made" in Paris.

By sheer good luck it just chanced one day that a far more powerful individual than any mere royal or social potentate happened to drop in at the Cercle Internationale. This was Villemessant, Editor of *Figaro*.

He had not listened to that music for five minutes, he had not watched its very embodiment in the vivid figure of Johann, before he realised that here was something wholly fine, exquisite, unique, something in short for him, Villemessant, to discover and present to Paris!

He invited the Austrian to call upon him at his office. "Monsieur Strauss" made haste to do so, with the result that the great newspaper man's intention was abundantly confirmed. Villemessant set about a Strauss campaign in the press, which could be favourably compared with anything of the sort embarked upon in modern times. Every paper in Paris followed his lead until to have seen and heard "M. Strauss qui a le diable au corps" became the latest and most imperious rage of the Exhibition. Strauss was presented again at the *Figaro* offices to everyone of note in art or letters, to such men as Flaubert, Rochefort, and to Dumas fils.

He returned these overpowering compliments by a dinner to the paper's staff for whom he expressly composed a polka. Monsieur Villemessant insisted upon paying for the very special wine drunk on this immense occasion, and promptly published the new dance as a Figaro supplement. The affair on either side waxed more and more enthusiastic until the public was swept completely off its feet, and for the future no concert at the Cercle could be concluded without that waltz of all waltzes whose very first bar now wrought the audience to a frenzy of delight.

"The Blue Danube" conquered Paris. "Mr. Strauss," wrote one admirer, "is a gentleman who dances his own waltzes and quadrilles with violin, arms, neck, shoulders and head. It is impossible for anyone to sit still; he would make the very pillars of the concert hall twirl round and dance."

The papers were full of this "succès fou". Villemessant knew how to exploit it to its utmost limit. Strauss was made in Paris.

From that time on we read of him "filling the rooms with melody", of "Halls of dazzling light where Strauss holds his midnight—nay, to-morrow morning—revelries", and this always and inevitably to the strains of "The Blue Danube".

"The Blue Danube" had conquered Paris.

It conquered the English princes.

Towards the end of May that "English family man and Parisian dandy", the Prince of Wales, turned up in Paris accompanied not by the Princess but by the Duke and Duchess of Manchester. The first act of H.R.H., after paying his compliments at the Tuileries, was to despatch a note to Hortense Schneider at the Variétés, asking her to have a proscenium box reserved for him that very evening. Otherwise the house was sold out. The Schneider gathered this crowned head to herself, together with a large number of similar trophies, with immense éclat. The whole court of the Grand Duchess of Gerolstein attended the ball given for Strauss at the Princess Metternich's. The Prince of Wales was soon enslaved by the music from Vienna.

"Whatever their Royal Highnesses did, they did thoroughly," wrote one of the English correspondents, "and ended up with a ball at the Tuileries. Perhaps on the whole this was the most magnificent and striking entertainment offered them. Strauss superintended the music, and very well he did it, though not better than Waldteufel. . . . It was admitted—and in Paris this is a great admission —that in quadrille, polka, waltz, or cotillon nobody could beat the two English princes. I wonder the younger escaped with his life. . . ."

As for Strauss, the company at such a ball as this judged the success of the music by the number of violin bows he broke in the course of the evening.

Nothing would do for the Prince of Wales after this but that Strauss and "The Blue Danube" should come to England.

So they did.

Strauss came on to London in the late summer of that year, and conducted a series of concerts at Covent Garden from August 16th to October 25th—the ancestors of the "Proms"—when his wife also frequently appeared and sang.

The *Illustrated Sporting and Theatrical News* published Frau Henrietta Strauss's portrait, and particulars of her life and training, all of which must have had much interest for the English music-loving public.

Turning back the clock, and turning back many, many pages of *The Times*, we come across the following announcement for Friday, 15th August, 1867.

"Covent Garden Concerts . . . Mr. Russell has secured the services of Herr Johann Strauss, a son of the Viennese Strauss of European celebrity.

"This gentleman, who strongly resembles his father in manner, seems also to possess a large share of those qualities which led to his father's renown. He conducts the Orchestra like his father, fiddle in hand, and joins in the passages of some importance. This he does with wonderful animation, accompanied by a certain amount of characteristic gesticulation which also has something to do with the general impression created.

" . . . That the future success of the Covent Garden concerts depends materially on him we think unquestionable."

There followed an announcement of the programmes to be given during this season, a mixed bag, including Rossini and Wagner. It would appear that the Concerts were under the general conduct of Signor Bottesini, but that "in order to give éclat (to them) Mr. Russell has engaged, solely for the dance music, the services of the renowned Johann Strauss from Vienna".

Johann generally conducted four times during each concert, and was enthusiastically encored over and over again night after night. The brilliant "Annen" polka with its delicious trillings and the "Morgenblätter" seem to have been the prime and irreplaceable favourites, but at a Mendelssohn Concert on 22nd August he also gave the "Tanz Signale". On a Wednesday, 18th September, he was billed to give his great choral waltz, "On the Beautiful Blue Danube", with full orchestra and chorus of male voices. On the 25th of the next month came his benefit and a perfectly intoxicating finale for his season.

"The most wonderful night of my life," he noted in his diary. "Adieu, geliebtes England." He composed a dance, "Erinnerungen an Coventgarten" (Memories of Covent Garden), in honour of his reception there. Decsey says that he embodied English folk-motives in this work, but as it is somewhat doubtful how Strauss found any opportunity to study these, the radio listener—if he should ever be regaled with the Erinnerungen—is in no position to judge how far he succeeded.

All the papers had been most enthusiastic, and had devoted many paragraphs and notices to the celebrated Viennese composer. It would be interesting to know where Johann and Jetty stayed in London, and what they thought of it.

As for the wonderful dance itself, the score was printed from copper plates at that time, each one of which furnished about 10,000 copies. Hundreds of these plates were required to fill the demand. Millions of copies were sent out from Vienna throughout Europe as well as to America and Australia. This in pre-radio days meant, of course, supreme success!

CHAPTER XI

STRAUSS returned to Vienna, to the great jubilation of the city, crowned with French and English laurels. And a year after "The Blue Danube" he wrote an even more beautiful piece, perhaps, called "Tales from the Vienna Woods". This is, indeed, a musical picture of sylvan beauty, of elusive sunlight in the undergrowth, of golden glades where gladsome woodland creatures gambol, of nymph-haunted glens, and mysterious enticing leafy vistas. In writing it the composer had in mind the city worker chained to desk and office all the week, those "slaves of business"—whether clerk or king—shut up within walls and streets, imprisoned in shops, warehouses, bureaux, who escape into the country only on Sunday afternoon. It made of the "Wiener Wald" a delicious seventh-day institution for the commercialised middle-class of Vienna, and enticed them to go holiday-making on the same wholesale scale as that of working Parisians off for the whole day to Meudon, St. Cloud or Vincennes.

Words by Hans Müller were set to this music, but it was song enough without them, and they were soon dropped, although occasionally we still hear them gloriously given by some coloratura soprano equal to such a task, upon the air.

Other well-known Strauss pieces, also brought out originally as songs for the Male Choral Society, belong to this period, such as "Künstlerleben" (Artists' Life), "Wein Weib und Gesang" (Wine, Woman and Song), and a whole series of polkas which, in Pesth and elsewhere, continually served to heighten a reputation already elevated enough.

Of "Freut euch des Lebens" Decsey amusingly tells us that, unlike most of the Strauss music, it scarcely won the sort of popularity which made a melody sung, hummed and whistled everywhere by everyone, until some words got tacked on to it which distinctly smacked of Lerchenfeld —*not* the most cultured suburb of Vienna—and which derived little from the tradition of Goethe! This was all of a piece with that shocking aspect of things frivolous which allowed the public, in Vienna, to go into ecstasies of delight over the notorious Pepi Gallmeyer dancing the can-can as Gretchen in a parody of Faust. Pepi was one of the stars of the Viennese stage at this time, and the Viennese stage was almost as bad if possible as the Parisian.

Strauss continued to fulfil his contract with the Russian Railway Directors, and to put in May to September every year at the famous Vauxhall in Pavlovsk. He wrote a great deal of music for these Russian occasions,[1] and seems to have had a very good time indeed, adulated by society, adored by the women, and treated like a king. He seems also to have had hectic love affairs and adventures of all sorts, which he both survived and escaped by return to Vienna, and to an apparently commonplace marriage with the Treffz. There is stuff enough in all this for a dozen screen plays.

Strauss wrote his "L'Inconnue" to the unknown lady who constantly sent him flowers (apparently for the most part, names as well as prayers, sighs, and vows, were attached to the rest), only at length to make heart-fluttering discovery as to who she really was!

[1] Such as Nikolaiquadrille, Warschauerpolka, Grosfürsten Marsch, Alexandrinen Polka, Alschied von Petersburg, Fürst Bariatinsky Marsch, Newa Polka, Aus dem Parolowskwalde, Slowianka Quadrille, Im russichen Dorfe, etc. etc.

It was all very hectic and very silly.

There was lots of fun in it too. Leibrock, Strauss' Secretary in Pavlovsk, had an immense amount of work to do, apart from his proper functions, in rushing about with love letters, and fabricating his chief's autograph to satisfy the multifarious demand for it.

It was just before he became Director of the Court Dance Music that Strauss accepted an invitation to appear and give a concert in the Royal Opera House in Berlin. His programme consisted of ten selections, but their number was fully doubled before the tumultuously enthusiastic audience would permit him to make his final bow. The occasion was one which he never forgot.

．　　　．　　　．　　　．　　　．

Time went on, crammed with work, but changes were at hand, after which Strauss's life took on an entirely different artistic complexion.

Her son's extraordinary attraction to Henrietta Treffz had been a bitter pill for his mother to swallow. She could not understand it, and for some time she had refused to let him bring this ex-mistress of a Jewish financier to see her. She was filled with astonishment, disappointment, prejudice and apprehension for the future. There was nothing about the Treffz or the Treffz history to commend them to Schani's devoted and self-sacrificing mother. Nevertheless he stood by his guns, and willy-nilly, the pair meant to marry. Strauss went off again, on one of his Russian seasons, and meantime the situation became easier in the Hirschenhaus. Frau Strauss evidently discovered for herself those qualities in Jetty which were to make her son completely happy (if only, alas, for a while), for she seems to have faced the inevitable, when it came, with equanimity if not with actual pleasure.

Schani left the parental home at length with her thanks for all he had been to her and it, and confided his welfare and his fortunes to another woman's hands. Two more sons remained, but with the course of time, and with all of them taking to the same profession, it was more or less inevitable that certain strains and conflicts and even rivalries should arise among the brothers. Frau Strauss obviously felt her day was over. She could no longer rule a happy musical roost.

She was deeply wounded. Like many another mother she had to realise that the costly devotion of half a lifetime counted for little with her son now. She had to ask herself if Schani had ever really known the bitterness of that devotion and that sacrifice. She spent most of the time in her own room. She was found there one day, sitting with her head fallen back upon the cushion of her chair. Anna Strauss was dead.

They laid her to rest in the Friedhof St. Marx; a great ball was cancelled which otherwise was to have been given in Vienna that night. The only one of the family who did not attend the funeral was her best beloved "Schani". Johann simply could not bear it! He had a horror of the stark reality of death, and of all the mystery beyond it. His silence, however, even more than his absence on this supreme occasion, was a deeper tribute to his mother's memory than any other he might have offered. But perhaps the one who felt her loss the most was the melancholy high-strung Josef. . . .

Only a week before this happened, on the 18th of February, 1870, Strauss had written "Neue Wien".

.   .   .   .   .

It has already been related how Johann was obliged on his breakdown in '53 to call upon his brother Josef to deputise for him with his orchestra. Although Josef at twenty-three had now settled down to his own chosen profession and was getting on well in it, he was also an admirable musician. He had already composed serious music for the piano, and like his other brother Edouard was a great admirer of classical literature.

When Johann came back after his rest cure with Tante Josephine and took stock of Josef's musical stewardship, his last misgivings, if he had ever had any, disappeared. Josef had proved himself true to the Strauss tradition.

In spite of some unfriendliness on the part of the critical musical press when he first appeared, Josef Strauss refused to let himself be intimidated. Called away from his plans and his blue prints, and pitched at a moment's notice from the status of a musical amateur to that of a professional, he plunged with his usual thoroughness into a course of study: he now took up instrumentation and the violin.

Unlike Johann who had left the Hirschenhaus, Josef continued to live there with his mother even after his marriage to Caroline Pruckmeyer, his "liebes einziges Weib Kathi", by whom he had one daughter. He seems to have given his wife little cause for the inevitable jealousies which were ultimately to be the ruin of Jetty Strauss's conjugal adventure.

Josef Strauss was a curious contradiction to Johann. Similarly gifted, the brothers differed very much in temperament. But of temperament as temperament both had their full share! Josef was tuned in the minor key, and showed his preference for this in most of his work, but Johann lived in the major. Josef was the better man. His moods, however, alternated from heights of Viennese gaiety to depths of gloom, which fact must have made him difficult to live with unless everyone else in the

Hirschenhaus was similarly afflicted, which seems highly likely.

Whatever Josef undertook he did with all his might. He was very modest about his qualifications and achievements. For his dreaded début with Johann's orchestra he wrote a waltz which he significantly called "The First and Last", and, astonished that a successor should be promptly demanded, followed it up with "The First after the Last".

For the next seventeen years Josef Strauss was to lead a life as fertile in production, as busy with engagements, and almost as popular as the head of the family himself. He did a great deal of original work both as conductor and as composer, and also in conjunction with Johann and with Edouard. Caricatures of the period show the three brothers skipping about arm in arm flourishing their fiddles, on the very lightest and most fantastic of toes.

Had Josef Strauss lived as long as Johann it is possible he might have been considered the finer musician of the two. Many critics considered him the most gifted of the three brothers. Some of his inspiration derives from Franz Schubert. He has been called the Schubert of dance music. He had not the faintest idea that any of his work would live, and yet his "Dorfschwalben" (Village Swallows), "Brennende Liebe" (Flaming Love), "Aus der Ferne" (From a distance), "Aquarellen", "Frauenherz", etc. etc., and other of his compositions deserve to rank with what is most lasting in his father's and his brothers' work. We sometimes hear one or another of Josef Strauss's dances on the air, but it is a pity we do not hear more. The famous "Pizzicato Polka" was a joint work of his and Johann's.

He soon made a name for himself in Vienna, and that with the most enthusiastic section of his brother's public. He supplied Johann's place, on occasion, at the Court

K

Balls, in the Redoutensaal, and in the Imperial Volksgarten. In fact he often accompanied or deputised for his brother on the Russian tours.

The third brother, Edouard, also devoted himself to music, and after 1859 was closely associated with the other two. But rifts appeared in the family lute, and towards the end of her life Frau Strauss had found it more and more difficult to maintain harmony in the Hirschenhaus. Johann and Jetty ranged themselves, out of the security of their own home, on the side of the melancholy and high-strung Josef, when, during one of his absences in Russia, Edouard suddenly asserted an independence of his own and decided to go on tour, without consulting either of his brothers. Josef wrote from Pavlovsk to his "liebe Kathi" in Vienna complaining that this sort of thing would seriously jeopardise their affairs with the publisher, Spina, and that if his mother countenanced Edouard's behaviour they had better give up their life in common in the Hirschenhaus, and he would be glad to contribute a yearly sum towards her support elsewhere. He was tired of the old arrangement. He was tired of being, himself, under the family thumb, and would gladly reorganise the orchestra and carry on for the future on his own account.

The Russian contract was not renewed, and Josef returned home in no very cheerful frame of mind. It was largely these troubles which told so severely on Anna Strauss that finally she sank under them and died. Her death was a great blow to this second son, and he survived her by but a few months. Josef was never strong. He was a confirmed smoker, and hated exercise in the fresh air. He suffered perpetually from headaches and fainting, and was always convinced that his own life would not be of long duration. Anna Strauss died in the February of 1870. Josef collapsed while directing a concert at Warsaw the following July.

Something suddenly went wrong in the orchestra—a careless first violin had overlooked a repeat, and chaos momentarily resulted—whereupon the conductor's nerve gave way. He was carried from the stage practically in a dying condition. His wife came hurriedly from Vienna, and they got him home, but there was a lesion in the brain, and he quickly sank and died. Fantastic rumours got about as to his demise. The press had it that he had been brutally manhandled by some drunken Russian officers because he declined an encore. But a paper had simply got hold of the wrong end of the stick, and muddled up names. Yet the scandal was immense, and yielded to no efforts at denial.

Oddly enough Josef had concluded a queer agreement with Edouard in 1869—just a year before his death—that whichever of the two should survive the other, was to destroy all his brother's orchestral arrangements. The music was not to fall into the hands of strangers. Edouard Strauss carried out the promise in 1907. He sent off in fact an entire repertory of the Strauss orchestra by wagon-loads to an oven factory in Vienna, and had the whole lot burnt. "He thus destroyed a piece of Viennese history itself, and robbed his native city of an irreparable musical treasure. . . ."

All Vienna grieved for the loss of Josef Strauss. "With him," says Lange, "went not only a great artist but a fine man of quite peculiar excellencies. Nothing was of more importance to him than the well-being of his own family, to promote which he freely sacrificed himself. He was much admired by some of the greatest of his contemporaries, among whom were Liszt and Rubinstein."

CHAPTER XII

JOHANN Strauss withdrew himself almost entirely, after the death of his mother, from public work in favour of his brothers, latterly, of course, in favour of Edouard. This synchronised with his entering upon a new sphere of work.

As a composer of waltzes and of dance music pure and simple, the first phase of his productivity came to a close with "Freut euch des Lebens", and with "Neue Wien". From that time onward he devoted himself to light opera in which the dances were but incidental numbers.

Neither Strauss senior nor Lanner had seriously contemplated writing for the stage. Nor did the idea of it at all appeal to the younger Johann. He felt no personal impulse to widen further the musical field which belonged so peculiarly to the house of Strauss, and which he, in particular, had done so much to beautify. A series of circumstances, rather than any ambition of his own, led, or over-persuaded him, in the new direction. Looking back over the period during which Johann Strauss composed sixteen Operettas, i.e. from 1871 to 1897, it is fair historical comment to say that perhaps it would have been better had he trusted his own instinct and stuck to his own particular musical last. This for two reasons. The first is, that unlike Offenbach who was particularly happy in his collaborators, Strauss rarely found the right librettist. His work for the stage was for the most part hampered by such verbal trash (except in very few instances) that the

148

productions were only tolerated for the sake of the music. The music itself might have disappeared, at times, had not this or the other revisionist done his best to extricate it and save it from the text. The whole story of Strauss's operettas is a story of radiant music pressed into the service of extraordinarily poor librettos.

Secondly, Strauss's public never expected and never tolerated anything from him but the thing to which it had always been accustomed—i.e. the very best and gayest and brightest of all the gay bright music ceaselessly poured forth by the army of musicians in Vienna. It gave him no chance to be serious, or to express any of the emotions save those of laughter, fun and frivolity. It practically amounted to this:—that Strauss's public demanded of him one eternal, bewitching dance. An overture which gàve no promise of this, however richly the promise might be redeemed later, filled a Strauss audience with consternation. Idolised as the master was, he yet served perhaps the most exacting public in Europe.

It was his writing for the Choral Society which came to form a natural transition from his first to his second phase. There was nothing particular to choose between a lot of people singing in black coats, and another lot of people singing in theatrical costume.

And it was a chance word of Offenbach's, probably spoken without any real intention, which sowed the seed of this new era, as far back as eight years previously. Offenbach came to the Vienna Carnival in 1864, a thin, ill-knit individual, with a huge Adam's apple, amazing whiskers, and piercing blue eyes behind a black rimmed pince-nez. He irradiated wit, and the Danubian metropolis was soon at his feet. Three pieces of his were appearing at the same time in different theatres. Offenbach delighted in Vienna (as did the expensive *petite amie* he brought with him from

Paris), and Vienna delighted in him. The result was that nearly a decade of French opera set in, accompanied by a deterioration of taste and morals which the city could really very ill afford.

However delicious the Offenbach music might be, there had been no necessity to introduce the cancan to the Austrian boards, or to infect a sufficiently susceptible society with that peculiar brand of "gaiety" which was the disgrace of the capital of the Second Empire. Princess Pauline Metternich did a good deal of harm in Paris, which she would not have dreamt of doing in Vienna—but Offenbach fully compensated for this.

His influence on Viennese music also was tremendous. The refinement of his technique and the force of his humour made an immense sensation. He settled down, very much at home, in Vienna, and was the life and soul of the collection of musical notabilities in his hotel in the Leopoldstadt, "The Golden Lamb". Should Johann Strauss appear in the offing, no one could be more complimentary to him than he.

His lightly thrown-off suggestion that Johann should try his hand at writing for the stage was probably nothing more than a Parisian compliment. This exaggerated praise offered Strauss by the man who was yet to write *The Tales of Hoffman* was not entirely sincere. No note of the Viennese composer's was ever allowed to be played in his fine residence in Paris, nor at his country place at Etretat. Offenbach scarcely meant his suggestion about Strauss writing operetta to be taken in earnest. He was secure enough in his own popularity and success to be able to afford this sort of gesture. What had he indeed to fear from any competition of Strauss's?[1]

[1] The story of German operetta, Herr Fritz Lange tells us, is more complicated than that of the French. The origin of it went far back to

The mere notion was laughable! What could this man do for the stage with his waltzes? And who was going to furnish him with a play? Some tup'ny hap'ny Viennese scribbler from the suburbs? . . . Laughable!

But there were music-lovers in this city who were jealous for the reputation of their native composers, and who looked on at Offenbach's sweeping triumph with some dismay. Among these was the Dalmatian, Franz von Suppé, himself director of a theatre orchestra, and popular composer for the stage. Vienna floated, indeed, in these days, in a

---

the somewhat rude comedy or farce accompanied with songs (Singspiel) which had always been popular among the Germans. This type of performance lent itself to every sort of alteration and development. Both music and text went through one change after another, in which it was always a question as to whether the broadly comic or the more artistic presentation of things should predominate. The affair was of its own genre, but difficult to define. Taste tended to change with the course of time, and the metamorphoses through which the "Singspiel" went until it blossomed into the "German operetta", were not easily to be distinguished one from another. With the death of Wenzel Müller in 1835 the Viennese lost their last popular "Singspiel" composer. Some of his songs had passed into popular possession and may still be sung to-day, but otherwise the artistic form he cultivated died out. After Müller's death his scores were stowed away in theatrical archives only to collect the dust. Then came the Revolution (1848) after which the Viennese cared little for the naïve genre of the native Singspiel, and ran after foreign gods. When Offenbach appeared he carried all before him, and the lightest of French music met with universal acclaim. Vienna had always welcomed foreign musical gods with open arms. Both French and Italian composers had felt themselves thoroughly at home on the banks of the beautiful blue Danube.

But the time had at length arrived when this immense popularity of music from Paris aroused competitive aspirations in the breasts of Vienna's own host of composers. One of the first to challenge Offenbach on his own ground was Franz von Suppé, himself a talented and versatile musician. This man grasped the essentials of the new type of performance, the opera bouffe, and saw the immense possibilities in it for all that was characteristically Viennese, high and low. Suppé was not so fortunate as the great common rival in his librettists, but at least he threw down the gauntlet to Offenbach, and Strauss ultimately picked it up, to create the German Operetta.

It has been said that the latter in comparison with French operetta was but a feeble middle-class caricature which "substituted cosiness for gaiety, stupidity for nonsense, and idle prattle for wit". This may very well have been true. None of Strauss's librettos will bear reading for a moment. And yet the Viennese product soon chased the French from the boards of the Kaiserstadt, and kept it crowded out for years.

very sea of melody occasioned by the musical competition excited by the Frenchman's success.

However anxious at this time the politicians and the Hofburg might be over the vexed Schleswig-Holstein question,[1] the public knew little and cared less about it, held as they were in the magic spell of Offenbach, Strauss and Suppé.

Seven years ('64–'71) and an interval of that appalling "dissonance in the symphony of life" which is war were to go by before anything more occurred to turn Johann's thoughts towards operetta.

It was natural enough that his wife should side with those friends of his who insisted he should attempt a more ambitious form. Jetty had years of stage experience behind her and could offer him a wealth of ripe advice and technical assistance, both as actress and as singer. No one admired Strauss the artist more than did his wife. No one believed more firmly in his capabilities.

Frau Jetty had indeed once brought up this identical question. It was when they were in Russia. Strauss was in excellent spirits. He had just paid a visit to the Director of a newly-formed Conservatorium of Music in St. Petersburg, an eminent musician called Anton Rubinstein, and had agreed with him, among other things, as to the promise of a certain favourite pupil, Peter Ilijtsch Tschaikowsky.

Later on, talking to Professor Bromberger, the question again came up as to the feasibility of Johann turning his attention to operetta. Everybody urged it upon him. Johann was most reluctant to entertain the idea, despite Jetty and the rest of his believers all put together. Whether this was due to the natural disinclination of a man no longer quite young, (and of one, moreover, who had made an entirely satisfactory success in his own sphere), to branch

---

[1] Palmerston said there were only three men who ever understood the Schleswig-Holstein question, the Prince Consort who was dead, a German professor who was mad, and himself who had forgotten all about it.

out more widely, and challenge comparison with men who
had long arrived on the boards—whether Johann's reluct-
ance was due to this or to downright ingrained Viennese
laisser aller—who can say?

But Frau Jetty was ambitious for him, and tenacious.
Back again in Vienna, and comfortably settled in a beautiful
villa at Hietzing (1870), this project of getting Johann to
envisage bigger things came again to the forefront of her
mind. She bethought herself of a ruse in order to force his
hand.

She knew that he was once supposed to have had a shot
at operetta . . . the thing had been called "Don Quixote".
She had a surreptitious look through his desk. There seemed
to be no end of stuff in it. Secretly she abstracted this,
that or the other promising-looking MS., and conveyed
them to Max Steiner, Director of the Theater-an-der-Wien,
who in his turn caused some lines to be written to suit
them, by his "Hausdichter".[1] Then came tentative performance. This turned out so admirably that both Frau
Strauss and the Director felt justified in inviting the composer to come down to the Theatre and be treated to a
rehearsal of his own work!

Surprised and amused himself, Strauss consented, only
to find that he really was impressed with the theatrical
possibilities of his music.

He opened tentative negotiations and learnt, incidentally,
that his old school friend Anton Langer, now a fairly successful and popular writer, would be quite ready to collaborate
as librettist. But, somehow or other, nothing came of this
suggestion. Strauss was only too conscious that at forty-
six it was late to hope to challenge the supremacy of a man
like Offenbach, who had long achieved the summit of success
in this field. He could not, however, altogether refrain

---

[1] Staff poet attached to the theatre.

from dallying with the idea. He brought himself to write the music for a couple of acts of a work called "Romulus", a parody on the founding of Rome, but flung it aside as disgusted with his efforts as with the text itself.

At last Suppé's own librettist, Josef Braun, offered him an operetta called "The Merry Wives of Vienna", which certainly took Strauss's fancy. He retired to his sanctum and rapidly and promptly, this time, set the whole to music. He wrote for the most part at night—that is to say he did the orchestration at night, for as far as composition itself was concerned, melodic inspiration took him unawares at any moment, anywhere. The slightest thing could occasion a musical idea, when Strauss would break off anything he might be doing, desert any company he might be in, to seize it and work it out. Right up to the last years of his life he never felt the need of prolonged sleep. He would smoke when he was at work. Sometimes he broke off to write a few urgent letters, or even to knock the billiard balls about. It was only during the afternoon that he took exercise, or gave himself up to an enjoyable game of Tarock with friends. He had a horror of what Lange amusingly calls "Salonlöwentum", of being a drawing-room lion, but much delighted in informal gatherings especially of his intimates.

When at work he liked to be alone—but to feel that there was somebody sympathetic about, like Jetty. This was a very different thing to being left alone. He would often call her to come, and sing the words for this or that passage upon which he was engaged, as he could never exactly remember them himself.

The score of "The Merry Wives" was completed and duly delivered at the theatre. But there the matter came to an unforeseen and abrupt full stop.

The Gallmeyer, Prima Donna at the Theater-an-der-Wien, in a fit of temperamental tantrums had had a flare-up with the Director and betaken herself to a rival, Treumann at the Karl Theater. It was impossible to produce the piece without her, and so no more was heard of it.

Strauss was good at cutting his losses. He could well afford to do so, for nothing taxed or exhausted his invention. A whole operetta could be thrown away, without making the least difference to him. The air was there still, and, as he said, his music came to him in the Viennese air. It was all about him like the sunshine and the flutings and carollings of the birds.

But Maximilian Steiner was convinced that all the ingredients for successful Viennese opera, humour and music, sharp mother-wit and laughable Austrian characteristics, existed in abundance at hand, and only needed to be well welded to drive the Parisian importation back whence it came. He refused to give in to the Gallmeyer, and set himself, together with a number of clever plagiarists and adapters—Vienna afterwards said forty—to concoct another libretto for Strauss. This was "Indigo and the Forty Robbers", in reality a mere hash-up from half a dozen sources of outworn nonsense, obviously reminiscent in spots of the very master it was designed to supersede. Steiner was right in hoping great things from native German operetta, but he made the big Austrian mistake here, of carrying things only half-way. It could redound neither to his nor to Strauss's advantage to be niggardly over the libretto, but this was what his procedure amounted to over "Indigo". The text was entirely unworthy of the music which Strauss undertook to write for it. But write he did, and the only person who entertained any doubts about the ultimate success of the piece was the composer himself.

All Vienna was on the tip-toe of excitement over the Master's new venture. On the evening of the 10th of February, 1871, the public stormed the Box Office at the theatre as it had stormed Dommayer's twenty-seven years before. The house was early sold out. Everyone who *was* anyone in music, art, or letters had managed to get in, together with a crowd of newspaper men and those inveterate first-nighters whom the Germans delightfully call "die Dabeiseinmüsser", (people in their own opinion so important that they absolutely *must* be there).

Strauss himself, driving down to the theatre, got a shock when he saw his name on the placards, and fell back, white, against the cushions. He was living over again some of the stage fright of his youthful début.

"The Theater-an-der-Wien was to all appearances a cosmopolitan opera house of the most flamboyant sort. It was built at the end of the eighteenth century for the man who concocted the libretto for Mozart's Zauberflöte. In the last days of Imperial Vienna it was a hotbed of fashion, but a good servant of music. At the back of the stalls, beneath the spacious diplomatic box, there was a standing place which gave a small and close-packed mass of people a perfect view of the stage. Part of this space used to be roped off and kept as a free standing place for 'K.U.K.'[1] officers in uniform."

The cast on this terrific occasion of Strauss's Première was excellent—old theatre-goers in Vienna remember to this day the name of the Geistinger (the prima donna)—and no pains had been spared with the scenario.

And, after all, "Indigo" had an immense reception. The music caught up the terrible libretto, and swept it to heights of success. The audience recognised their idol in

---

[1] Kaiserlich und Königlich—imperial and royal—i.e. Austrian and Hungarian. From *Vienna*. E. Crankshaw.

every note and cadence, and acclaimed him to their enthusiastic hearts' content. Since Wagner had come into his own in Vienna with the first performance of the "Meister-singers" at the Court Opera that same month and year, nothing had occasioned such tumults of applause.

The musical press had a great deal to say. One of the few critics of any real cultural pretensions hailed Strauss as a future and satisfactory substitute for the great Offenbach himself, although the "music pope", Eduard Hanslick, who made a point of never praising anyone save Brahms, found the piece too long, and would only admit, later, that he enjoyed it better after he had heard it more than once.

The story of Strauss's first operetta is not a long one. As "Indigo" it soon disappeared.

But there were not wanting those admirers of the Viennese master who were eager to make attempts to save the music in spite of the text. In Berlin the editor of the paper called *Kladderadatsch* did such clever things with the latter, thanks to much blue pencil and a fanciful invention of his own, that the piece enjoyed a warm reception there. For an equally successful Paris version it had been imperative to include "The Blue Danube". So many experiments were made by way of doing something, somehow, with this unfortunate libretto, and so many new titles were suggested for it, that at last an entirely new story was fitted to the score, and Strauss' first venture for the stage re-emerged as "A Thousand and One Nights".

But even so it was practically soon forgotten—and by no one with less regret than by the composer.

Strauss was snowed under, now, with libretti from all quarters. He wasted little time upon them. None of them came up even to "Indigo", and of "Indigo" he had had quite enough!

CHAPTER XIII

"THE FIRST NECESSITY OF MAN IS TO BE HAPPY", '72

NEXT, America! Strauss Vater had dreamed of it, Strauss Sohn was to conquer it. . . .

Hardly had he recovered somewhat from the fatigues and excitements of the production of his first work for the stage, than he was thrown into still greater excitement by one of the most flattering invitations of his career.

Boston was preparing an immense musical festival to celebrate a "World's Peace Jubilee" from June 17th to July 4th in the summer of 1872. Together with a number of other European musical celebrities, including Mr. Dan Godfrey from England, the Committee invited the celebrated ex-Hofballmusikdirektor Herr Strauss, of Vienna, to come and add lustre to the great occasion. The promoters offered him a fee of a hundred thousand dollars, free transport and hospitality for himself and his wife, a valet and a lady's maid.

However loath Johann might have been to contemplate so long a journey, and what was much worse, so long an absence from his beloved Vienna, there was no refusing an offer like this. Something was due to the very fame which had crossed the Atlantic and preceded him. Much was due to Jetty. She threw the whole weight of her influence on the side of acceptance, and nothing remained for the Master but to allow himself to be persuaded.

The little party sailed or steamed, or at that time did both, from Bremen on the first of June, 1872.

A great super-liner at that time meant a ship of some 5,000 tons. Whether she was driven by paddle wheels or screws, she also carried sail, which was set in favourable weather. Under any circumstances she was a roller and a plunger. Nor were her appointments to be compared with those of transatlantic travel to-day. The dining and other saloons were situated towards the stern, and being completely surrounded by cabins, had little or no ventilation. An American traveller of the period wrote that "the cleanliest steamer abounds in fumes". In the fairest weather it was necessary to have racks on the tables with compartments for each dish, yet in spite of this the breakage of crockery was enormous. There was little comfort on deck . . . no chairs, and no shelter save that to be got in the lee of the smoke stacks. The passengers' cabins were small and the berths narrow and springless. At midnight the bull's-eye lanterns and oil lamps which did duty as ships' illuminants were extinguished, leaving the passengers in darkness. Warming arrangements of some sort were sometimes to be discovered in the public rooms, but nothing was done about the cabins.

Notwithstanding the rigours of the adventure, which to Johann and his companions seemed splendid enough, everything went like clockwork, and the weather must have been propitious, for nobody who mattered seems to have been seasick. There was even a band on board, the band of the First Prussian Guards, who were to make a tour in the States, so that night after night the passengers danced to the strains of Strauss waltzes.

The trip lasted about fourteen days. The Strausses landed at New York and hastened on to Boston. The city gave a public reception to the distinguished continental musicians on Monday, June 17th. Johann himself was welcomed with "Yankeehaften Grimasse"—truly American gestures. Every street displayed gigantic hoardings with placards showing Strauss in a king-like attitude, bestriding the globe and ruling it with a fiddle bow in place of a sceptre. The people went half wild with enthusiasm, and such stirring scenes took place that he hardly knew whether to throw himself into the midst of the mêlée, or to flee for his life.

According to his contract he was to play at fourteen concerts, in a vast timber hall or palace which had been specially built for the purposes of the Festival. It was capable of seating a hundred thousand people, and the orchestra could accommodate twenty thousand musicians. A picture of it reminds one somewhat of the Crystal Palace on the occasion of some extra big musical festival. There was a vast organ built up at the back of a steep stage which spanned the entire width of the hall as far as the wide sloping galleries on either side. The roof, half hidden with serried loops of bunting, was supported by four widely spaced avenues of slender pillars hung with long variegated flags.

Strauss was filled with consternation at the mere sight of it. This was no place for music!

There was no help for it, however; Americans apparently thought of music in these terms. A hasty rehearsal—it was all they gave him—confirmed his worst impressions. Strauss was so appalled with the whole thing that it was as much as he could do not to throw up his contract then and there. He foresaw nothing ahead of him but a fantastic catastrophe.

Fortunately for the Bostonians and for everybody, Strauss was not the only continental lion who had been invited to grace the celebrations. Franz Abt Bülow and Verdi had also been confronted with the shock of the Boston Concert Hall in Back Bay, and had survived it. The first-named now did all he could to fortify and to pacify the Waltz King. But for Bülow, Strauss would have turned tail and fled.

On the evening of his first appearance the vast place was absolutely packed out. All sorts of imposing ceremonies had

been taking place since the morning, and the whole city
looked to Strauss at night to crown them. Six hefty con-
stables were required to forge a way for him, followed by
his man carrying the fiddle. The din was indescribable and
cheers rent the air without mercy or cessation. The women's
eyes followed the graceful, black, shock-headed figure here,
as they followed it in Paris and Vienna, with an idolising
curiosity.

The orchestra was filled with twenty thousand instru-
mentalists and singers. The conductor's stand was a kind
of wooden tower. Strauss scrambled somehow to the platform at the top, and beheld the sea of faces before him,
on either hand, and behind, with a desperate sinking of
the heart. He never cursed this American enterprise as
he cursed it at this moment. Oh! to be back in dear Vienna
away, away, three thousand miles and more away!

Of all ghastly things that were to happen on this ghastly
evening, his "Blue Danube" was to be sung by a hundred
thousand throats, American throats, at once. And he had
to conduct them! If by any heaven-sent chance his band
of sub-conductors, a hundred strong, taking the cue from
his own upraised arm, managed to get them off the mark
with anything like unison, it would be tempting Providence
to hope that they would make any kind of a respectable
finish. Strauss nerved himself for a cataclysmic failure.
If poor Josef had collapsed—dying—in Warsaw because
of a momentary chaos in his orchestra, we can be sure
Johann stared death (if only musical death) in the face
when his concert in Boston was opened by cannon shot!
But so it was, and by this sign, his hundred sub-conductors
were suddenly sprung upon the sight of the audience, with
a hundred batons awaiting the signal from their chief.
At last it came. . . .

The Witches' Sabbath broke loose. . . .

L

"I could only hear the people immediately round me," Strauss said afterwards, "there was no question of giving a performance in any artistic sense. How on earth was this row ever to be brought to an end? I shall never forget what I went through to the last day of my life. My chief concern was to wind up in some sort of style if it were humanly possible. Thank God I brought it off *somehow* and then they fell to applause and cheering." It was enough to raise the roof. Strauss dared to breathe once more, and felt like a swimmer who had only just managed to find the ground again under his feet in time.

The success was terrific, but so also must have been the strain.

This is what the Boston Musical critics had to say about it all next day:

"It is impossible to judge of extraordinary events by ordinary rules. Things without precedent must be criticised from a different point of view, and upon more general principles than apply to subjects with which we are familiar. The Jubilee music must be judged in this way."

Of the opening performance the *Herald* said, "The chief honours from a strictly musical point of view were carried off by Herr Strauss whose activity, firmness, and judgment, make him a model conductor. . . . He has, apparently, not an idle muscle in his body while he is conducting."

Vast concerts were given every day during the Festival, at each of which Strauss appeared and became a "victim of the encore nuisance which attained proportions little short of monstrous".

Some wit wrote:

"They have again in solo Peschk or Leitner,
    And as for that Herr Strauss
    The roar they raise for him's a perfect frightner
    And threatens to unroof the quaking house."

This was not to be wondered at, since one of the Waltzes Johann wrote in Boston, his New Jubilee Waltz, closed with a cheery arrangement of the "Star Spangled Banner" in waltz time!

During the Jubilee somebody published a daily comic paper full of Jubilee items and witticisms and remarks. Strauss's name—and an amusing drawing of his back, whilst conducting—frequently occurred in it. "Herr Strauss, Franz Abt, and the other distinguished musical strangers among us, have been the recipients of innumerable attentions from citizens during the past ten days. They have been promenaded, serenaded and lemonaded to almost any extent."

The "adorable Strauss", as he was called, gave all his most popular pieces, "Morgenblätter", "Wein Weib und Gesang", "Neue Wien", "Pizzicato Polka", "Circassian March", "Künstlerleben", to say nothing of "The Blue Danube", over and over and over again. Strauss "the mercurial", "the magnetic", "the irresistible", with his "electrical effect", his "dazzling and brilliant manner": Strauss, the "high potentate of chassey and forward two" was King of the revels, of course, at the great ball which was given on the evening of June 26th. The Feuilleton waxed eloquent over a description of the lace, ribbons, glove, fan and flower wreckage of that ballroom next morning.

"We really must object," it said, "to Herr Strauss and Mr. Dan Godfrey driving Boston waltz mad."

On the following day it was noticed that Strauss had sustained some injury to his right arm, for during the usual concert he conducted with his left, and did not play.

Meanwhile New York was excessively jealous of this musical tornado at Boston and wrote unforgivably rude things about it. This did not, however, prevent Strauss receiving an invitation to go thither at once, at the end of the Festival. He was said to have demanded a fee of $1,200 a night.

Indeed, the very morning after the first Boston uproar the Viennese master was beset by an army of impresarios who promised him all California, (this was in the gold rush days), for a tour of America.

Apparently nothing, not even the wealth of all California, was inducement enough to Strauss to go through quite such an experience again. He kept his American contract manfully, but he did not extend or renew it.

He performed at fourteen great concerts in Boston, and "in response to universal request" directed an orchestra of three hundred musicians at the ball. He closed what can only be described as his American campaign with four big concerts in the Opera House at New York. His success was such that it may be said without contradiction "that Strauss was the first King America was willing to crown".

He had made his will before leaving home, which act, under the circumstances, was a highly prudent one! It was granted to Europe, however, to see him back. He landed there again safely on the 13th of July, loaded down with American honours and dollars. He was not, though, to proceed directly to Vienna. Cholera had broken out in the Kaiserstadt, and the news of it gave Strauss a terrible shock. He had a morbid horror of sickness, disease—and death. He would always avoid passing a hospital or a cemetery, if possible. No one dare to mention these things in his presence.

Instead, therefore, of proceeding to Austria, Strauss decided to accept an invitation which was awaiting him on landing, to go to Baden-Baden and give some concerts there. No sooner was this arrangement concluded, than the great Viennese master took it into his head to play the spoiled Darling of the Gods—as indeed he had now become.

By courtesy of the Director of the Historical Collections of the City of Vienna.

STRAUSS THE YOUNGER CONDUCTING IN THE VOLKSGARTEN.

With a very good show of truth he declared that his American experiences had been so much too much for him that he must really visit Schwalbach first, and remain there a fortnight to recuperate. The Royalties at Baden-Baden must simply wait.

Immense perturbations ensued. Responsible individuals dashed from Baden-Baden to Schwalbach to make the most vehement, the most despairing representations to the capricious musician. They hit, of course, upon the right argument at last when they hit on the argument of the pocket. The Musical Director to the Grand Ducal Court called him a fool for turning his back on two thousand francs an evening!

Whereupon Johann gave way.

He set off with Herr Katzau and Jetty next day, travelling in a spacious and comfortable carriage. But when they reached Mainz he was so charmed with the place that nothing would induce him to resume the journey. The Director and Jetty, again, used every possible endeavour to bring him to see reason. The utmost they could do was to get him as far as Heidelberg.

Jetty and Katzau prevailed however the following day, and the party finally arrived at Baden-Baden.

So that was that!

In the course of the next few days Strauss was to be seen sauntering in the gardens of the Casino chatting in the liveliest fashion with one of his most ardent admirers, the Emperor William I.

Before he left the Grand Duchy, indeed, both the Kaiser and the Grand Duke inflicted upon him (although it was no infliction to Johann), a couple of high-sounding Orders as marks of their particular esteem.

He did not escape the temptations in Baden-Baden, which turned a good many heads more weightily crowned than his own. He succumbed, an easy victim, to the tables. Katzau's warnings and remonstrances fell on deaf ears. The moment the gaming rooms were opened, Strauss gave himself up to Roulette.

He lost—prodigiously.

So much, no doubt, for a good many of the American dollars.

But that was no great matter. Mountains of lucrative work loomed ahead of him. A second operetta, now well in hand, must be brought to completion, and the project of a huge International Exhibition—the first and last— to be held in Vienna the next year, promised to keep him busier than ever.

As has been already told, after "Indigo" Strauss had been snowed under by librettos. It was a curious thing that in a city swarming with talent like Vienna, no writer could be found to play Gilbert to Johann's Sullivan. The only one who might have adequately filled this rôle was Ferdinand Kurnberger, the man who had written the text for Schumann's "Manfred". But he was not in the swim of things theatrical in Vienna at that time—and he died too soon. It was largely owing to the fact that a Habsburg public too easily allowed itself to be divorced or diverted from all matters of serious general or political import, that little remained with which her theatrical artists could busy themselves but the lightest nonsense. For a long time parodies of classical themes or masterpieces had been all the rage on the Viennese boards. Ridicule of the Olympian, like Offenbach's "Orpheus in the Underworld", had set in by way of reaction to the stiff and dignified classicism of a previous vogue. But both these styles now belonged to the past, and the task before Strauss was to substitute something indigenous to the spirit of Vienna.

After his first impulse to sweep aside the textbooks

submitted to him in such numbers from all quarters, Strauss thought better of it, and gave himself up with much earnestness to the serious quest for a good libretto. Nevertheless he lacked two or three essentials for the task, firstly, any real idea of what exactly it was he wanted, secondly literary training, thirdly personal theatrical experience. A host of advisers and consultants, including Jetty, probably muddled him more than they helped him in all three respects. He was prone to imagine that in the case of two alternatives the text another man might select would prove to be just the very one he, with the first option on it, ought to have chosen for himself. He had no gift at all, as far as his text was concerned, of detecting a "sure thing". He compared and considered, laid aside the likelier from the impossible, set a few passages to music—declined the lot—only to return to the task less qualified than at the outset to make up his mind. At last Director Steiner suggested something of Josef Braun's. And Josef Braun, medical student turned journalist, could very possibly have written something really distinctive and worthwhile for Strauss, had he not fallen back on the common trick of the day and borrowed from the French. He read Sardou, and concocted a play for Strauss with "Piccolino" running through his head. He called it "Carnival in Rome", and the Master was relieved at last to perceive possibilities. The thing composed. It stimulated a flow of musical ideas.

Strauss accepted it and set to work.

The story was simple enough, and the heroine as hackneyed and resourceful an innocent as ever bid for the operatic public's sympathies.

A young painter, Arthur Bryk, afoot in Switzerland, comes across an ingenuous Alpine milkmaid, paints a picture of her at prayer, and falls in love with her. Strauss thought there might be quite a lot in this for him—mountain backgrounds and idyllic village scenes. True, painting did not suggest much, but love-making did. There could be any amount of that. Of course Arthur promises the maiden marriage and then goes away and forgets her. Here, again, what was lacking in originality could certainly be made up in melody. Arthur betakes himself to Rome, and in his temperamental adventures there against a splendid background, Strauss found material enough for a dozen "Artists Lives". But "Marie" is no Gretchen left to face a tragedy. She is a young woman of decision and enterprise. She dresses up as a Savoyard youth—immense opportunity for the music—and sets off after her truant lover. She finds him in Rome, gets herself enrolled among his students undetected, wins him from undesirable scenes and seductresses, all of which admirably suited Strauss, and conducts him with unconscious Shavian guile to the predestined altar.

Anyhow they need be neither sticks nor clowns, these two, Arthur and Marie. The operetta could be conceived in lyric or in comic vein or both. Strauss felt he could do more here than rely upon the three-four beat for his effects. He could do something finer than "Indigo" with this, something deeper, and better worth while.

He wrote his second operetta, which was produced at the Theater-an-der-Wien on the 1st of March, 1873, two months before the opening of the great Exhibition. It was an immediate and immense success. Marie Geistinger was the prima donna. She seems to have delighted the Viennese by her beauty and her charming voice, much as Miss Grace Moore delighted everybody in her glorious "One Night of Love". But the old-fashioned photographs of the supposedly disguised maiden as an art student in Rome belong so absurdly to the ridiculous theatrical convention of the 'seventies, that they badly destroy our attempt to realise the magic which enraptured her conductor and her audiences at that date.

In "Carnival in Rome" Vienna possessed an opera worthy of the Exhibition year, and the house was sold out night after night.

CHAPTER XIV

VIENNA IN '73

THE International Exhibition at Vienna which had already been two or three years in planning, opened with much pomp and imperial circumstance on the 1st of May, 1873. It was truly a magnificent affair, and covered five times the area of the Paris Exhibition. Looking out N.E. over Vienna—now a very modern Vienna with tree-planted boulevards and well-paved or macadamised thoroughfares—from a spot above the Burgtor, the Exhibition lies some three miles away, in the Prater. Immediately in front, below, is the great, rectangular, heterogeneous mass of the Hofburg itself, flanked to the left by the umbrageous Volksgarten, and to the right by the Hofgarten. In the midst of the crowded streets and great blocks of buildings in the compressed inner city, is the Stefanskirche, with its beautiful spire. Many churches stand up out of the great sea of rectangular buildings, catching the eye at all points. The lines of the great boulevards are easily to be traced. On the left there is the vast block of the Rossauer barracks. Beyond the great Ringstrasse the city opens out, and becomes increasingly spacious and unrestricted as it fans towards its fringe. The river Wien is threaded through it, and the Danube Canal draws a long line of demarcation between the Leopoldstadt and the plain, meadows, and green hills in the distance. Away to the right is the Prater Stern and the three-mile-long Allée, together with the Exhibition, an immensely long, narrow, rectangular building, with a vast number of flanking galleries built on either side at right angles, and a Rotunda in the middle three times the size of the dome of St. Paul's. This is the "Industrial Palace" in which the treasures of the world are being transported, unpacked, and erected at the date of the opening. For the Exhibition is still far from complete. The weather on this 1st of May, 1873, is not good-tempered. It is gusty and fitful.

Nevertheless a very brilliant concourse of royalties and titled notabilities of Europe at that amazing and now forgotten date accompanied the Emperor, the Empress and the Crown Prince Rudolf to the inauguration ceremonies. The proceedings began with a performance in the Rotunda, of music specially written for the occasion, after which Baron von Schwartz Senborn, the Director General of the Exhibition, presented an address to the Emperor, inviting him to open it. Someone presented a tight and very circular cabbage of flowers by way of a bouquet to the imperial Elizabeth, whose preposterous hat, perched atop of a massy chignon all her own, and still more preposterous dress, one immense complication of draped and furbelowed and caught-up bustle, could yet do nothing to detract from her more than queenly dignity.

All Vienna was there, the women in the height of the prevailing amazing fashion, the men in every gorgeous uniform with which military or any other service could dazzle the day. And all Europe was there, too. People had been streaming into Vienna from London, Paris, Berlin, Madrid, for weeks. All the hotels were full. The city was prepared to give itself up to such an unceasing round of festivities, from imperial and state affairs, down to the balls and dinners of private hostesses, as had not been seen since the Congress. There was Gounod at the Opera, and Strauss at the Theater-an-der-Wien.

In fact, there was Strauss everywhere. . . .

Quarrels, however, with his brother Edouard had done

something to destroy for Johann the pleasure of the success of the "Carnival in Rome", and of the heady doings at the Exhibition.

Edouard was now directing the "Strauss Orchestra", which had become his own since the Waltz King's more or less complete withdrawal to the composer's study, and had greatly augmented it in the confident expectation of being called upon for its services at the International Exhibition. Greatly to his chagrin he learnt that, instead of this, the President had engaged an orchestra from Elberfeld under its own Director Langenbach, and that Johann was to conduct it alternately with this gentleman.

It was a bitter pill for Edouard. He was a highly gifted musician, executant, conductor and composer, a typical Strauss, but with the Strauss genius left out. No degree of the very considerable popularity and esteem he had won for himself, both abroad and at home on his own account, could compensate him for perpetually living in the shade of Johann. He was morosely jealous of his brother. He had already written a good deal of music, some of it in collaboration with Josef, or with Josef and Johann together, but he was not possessed of the cheerful spirit which was so characteristic of every dance of the latter's. He was a typical dandy of the period, with a shock of well-tended black hair, and an imperial moustache. He was a well-known and much-ogled figure in Vienna, and went about in light-coloured gloves and a yellow overcoat.

Edouard had taken up music, somewhat like Josef, on second thoughts. His first ambitions had been literary, and he was, perhaps, the best educated of the three brothers, possessing good Greek and Latin, and a knowledge of two modern languages other than German. He had studied theory under Preyer and Sechter, the violin under Franz Amon, and the harp, at Johann's suggestion, under

Parish-Alvars and Zamara. His first public appearance was at a monster ball given in the Diana Saal in February, 1859, when all three Strauss brothers directed an orchestra apiece and united their efforts for the final quadrille.

He had come in the course of time to take a great deal of this sort of work off Johann's shoulders. Together with Josef, he directed the Strauss orchestras both in Vienna and abroad until the year 1870. He was a brilliant first violin, and played the characteristic Strauss music, whether his brothers' or his own, absolutely faithfully in the Strauss tradition, that is to say faithfully to the imperious injunctions of Johann. In this respect he differed entirely from the innumerable military band masters who imitated it and made of it merely a thing of mass consumption.

Edouard was a married man in 1873 with two boys still under ten years of age. He was anxious to provide well for his family which seems to have cost him all he could earn, and this may have had something to do with the trouble that broke out between him and Johann over the music for the International Exhibition.

The festivities attendant upon the great opening in May drew enormous crowds to the Exhibition and particularly to the concerts. Johann wrote a choral waltz especially for the occasion—"Bei uns z'Haus'" which was the Viennese people's welcome to the thousands of strangers from abroad. Vienna was "At Home" to the world, and Johann was her first Receptionist. Strauss directed the orchestra, as has been said, alternately with Langenbach, but, after the resignation of the President who was responsible for this arrangement, Edouard, having come to an understanding with his brother in the meantime, found himself able to carry out his cherished plan. The Strauss Band was now to play at the Exhibition on the same footing with the Langen-

bach, so all went merry as a wedding bell—until the crash!
—and after.

Only a week after the great opening a terrible bank failure
took place in Vienna, which precipitated a widespread
monetary crisis. The city was thrown into desperate pertur-
bation. Wealthy men found themselves beggared overnight.
Endless undertakings were instantly ruined. For the moment
dance halls and concert rooms were forsaken, only foreigners
continued to throng the galleries of the Exhibition. Everything was plunged into gloom. "Vienna had invited the
world to a wedding feast which had turned into a funeral."
The Bourse collapsed. A thousand swindling enterprises
which had been carrying on for years came tumbling down
and sweeping all before them. A surging mass of men gone
practically mad howled for the blood of those responsible,
and magnates of the Stock Exchange had to fall back on the
police and the military for protection. On the "black
Friday" in that week began a series of suicides of those
suddenly reduced to penury. As a band went by the Bourse
playing "The Blue Danube", the crowd yelled after it that
folk enough were flinging themselves into the river! The
ruin of whole classes of the population was accompanied
by terrible scenes in this drama of finance.

Nevertheless the disaster soon fell out of the first page
of the European papers as "news". The measures of relief
which, they reported, were "promptly adopted", so far
ameliorated conditions that the Exhibition, at any rate,
survived the setback. By June a glorious summer was in
full swing, everything on the Prater was at last in final order,
and the season set in in good earnest.

Johann Strauss came to the general rescue with his
infallible panacea, a new Waltz. He wrote "Wiener Blut"
to cheer the people up, and succeeded. It was impossible
to be miserable long in Vienna in 1873. When the flood

of consternation ebbed away, carrying its wrecks with it, the sun broke out again, and the rainbow that was Strauss was found spanning the city. It was freely admitted at the time that Johann's operetta played a great part in helping people back to normality after the shock. Throughout the whole of this "Dance Macabre", when hundreds were forced to seek the pawnshops who had hardly known of their existence before, they betook themselves thither managing to hum or whistle amusingly appropriate snatches from the "Carnival in Rome".

Then towards the end of this year, 1873, a curious sequel of theatrical negotiations resulted in Johann Strauss' acceptance of an undertaking which, together with "The Blue Danube", was to place him among the immortals— of his kind.

Herr Steiner, the Director of the Theater-an-der-Wein, had bought a new operetta. It was a vaudeville from Paris, a thing originally called "The Prison" by Benedix, but remodelled by Offenbach's famous librettists, Meilhac and Halévy, and renamed "The Supper at Midnight".

Steiner, however, was not sure about this venture. It was very French, and would not easily transplant to Vienna. He tried to sell it to Direktor Jauner of the Karl Theater, but without success. It came back on his hands. At length, however, the publisher Lewy suggested the thing might suit Strauss, if it was knocked about a bit, and adapted. Steiner agreed, and entrusted his vaudeville to two clever collaborators, Haffner and Genée, who were to do their best with it. Haffner, whose tragic name occurs here for the first time in the story of Strauss, was a hard-driven hack writer for the Karl Theater, pledged to turn out twelve comedies a year. Genée, from now on destined to be long associated with the composer of "Die Fledermaus", was himself already a writer, composer, and conductor of some celebrity.

These two men set to work on "The Supper at Midnight", and did immense things with it. They followed the original "Prison" up to a point, but then turned and twisted things considerably, introduced new figures, invented good theatrical excuses for their intrusion, and contrived that the principal singers should never have occasion to linger long off stage. They made a thoroughly workmanlike thing of the whole; it was well constructed and gave illimitable scope to the man who was to be invited to write the music for it. Moreover it scintillated with fun, and had taken on a typically Viennese complexion. It lent itself to a gay and attractive "decor", and most important of all, the *dramatis personae* were living human beings instead of conventional puppets. It was sheer middle-class comedy, not to be too severely compared with "Figaro" or the "Barber of Seville" perhaps, but excellent as a "Faschings-buch" (a play for carnival time) in Vienna.

Direktor Steiner submitted it to Strauss. Johann was passionately fond of animals, of well-bred horses and dogs in particular. But he greatly disliked nocturnal creatures, and those which live in murky nooks and corners. Rats, snakes, bats, etc., could not be numbered amongst his friends. And yet the title of the textbook which now lay before him was "Der Fledermaus" (The Bat)!

At first he was not at all pleased. He considered the name "The Bat" far-fetched, unnatural. But everything else about the libretto delighted him. Here, he felt, was something really good, really what he wanted, something with which he could grip the Viennese opera-going public.

He accepted it, and flung himself into the work of setting "Die Fledermaus" to music with the ardour of a boy. He shut himself up in his study, away from the whole world. A fresh spring was blossoming and burgeoning in his mind, and no second must be lost in gathering its fragrant flowers.

Night was turned into day and his pen flew over the paper
without rest or intermission. Jetty saw to it that no dis-
turbance came near him. Visitors were strictly taboo.
Only Director Steiner, long counted among his intimates,
and Genée, appeared from time to time in the Hietzinger
Villa to enquire after the progress of the work. The latter
was full of original and happy ideas, and since Strauss always
had plenty of views of his own which Genée meticulously
respected, collaboration between the two boded everything good for the play.

We can imagine it was a very happy time in the Hietzinger
villa during the composition of the "Fledermaus". Strauss
was surrounded by the gaiety which scintillates through the
operetta. Frau Jetty fully appreciated its possibilities,
and we can be sure she was ever at her husband's call to
sing over for him this, that or the other of the bewitching
arias with which it is so full. Jetty was the first Rosalind
and the first Adèle. Very probably Strauss took her advice
here and there as that of an experienced singer, with regard
to vowels on high notes, and to the more ambitious vocal
passages. Even at this date composers were beginning to
complain that there were few really accomplished coloratura singers to be obtained.

Strauss was doubtful as to the good taste, or at least as
to the compatibility, of the comic passages at the end with
the Prison Governor, and the tipsy Warder Frosch. He had
to be urgently overpersuaded to put in a scene which proved
in the event, and has proved ever since, to be one of the
most successful parts of the operetta. "The Bat" would
be half the thing it is without that ridiculous fun at the
end. The Director knew exactly to whom he would confide the various parts. He thought of the Geistinger for
the lady's maid Adèle, and of an actor called Friese as
Frosch.

M

Strauss made a great point of the stage setting, the dressing of the piece. He wanted everything to be of the newest and the best. Director Steiner was appalled at the prospective costliness of the whole business, but Strauss managed to over-ride him here as fortunately for the piece, as Steiner and Jetty together had over-ridden him about the prison scene!

And so it went! In six weeks the work was finished. Or, to be more exact, in forty-two nights Strauss wrote the entire score.

CHAPTER XV

STRAUSS was fifty-one when he wrote "Die Fleder-maus". He had reached that high point in his career, when he could look both behind him and in front of him with self-congratulation. But he had also reached a point when it became impossible to allow any silver strand to appear in his swarthy locks. It was necessary for Johann to remain young. Accordingly, he did so. . . .

His masterpiece was achieved, and however good much of his subsequent work may have been it never reached this height.

The "Fledermaus," or parts of it, particularly the Overture, and some of the incidental waltzes and polkas, are often to be heard over the Radio. For those who have never seen this brilliant and butterfly-like operetta, but only listened to the score, it is necessary, briefly to relate the slight but complicated story, scintillating with irresponsible fun and effervescing (like the champagne in which it is drenched), with sheer, impossible nonsense.

A cheerful-minded gentleman of too much leisure and too independent means, Herr Gabriel von Eisenstein, has committed some trivial offence—struck a Sheriff's officer with a whip and called him a donkey, for which he has to go to prison for a little while.

On the day on which the action begins he is still at large, but bound in honour to betake himself to the gaol and give himself up in the course of the evening.

His wife, Rosalind, is discovered alone in their apartment, much exercised by the fact that an old-time admirer of hers, a tenor, Alfred, has turned up again, and is, at that moment, passionately warbling in the garden below and compromising her with his top A. The maid, Adèle, has just asked permission to go out and visit a sick aunt—she really wants to attend a ball—and has been refused.

Alfred reaches the Eisensteins' rooms, and bursts in on Rosalind. She tells him she is married; that her husband is just about to go to prison; and only succeeds in getting rid of him by promising to receive him again after Gabriel's departure. "I wish to goodness he wouldn't sing,"[1] she says. "His dialogue I can resist, but with such a top B I am powerless."

Strauss, of course, made the most of that top B.

Eisenstein appears with his lawyer, Blind, in a hefty operatic temper because the latter's pleadings have only succeeded in lengthening, instead of shortening, his sentence by three days. The whole amusing passage between Gabriel and Blind and Rosalind antedates the best Gilbert and Sullivan nonsense. Another character comes in just after this, a Dr. Falke, a boon companion of Eisenstein's, who yet has a secret grudge against him for a prank played in the past, and who fully intends to get his own back in good time. The time would seem to be at hand. Eisenstein is due at the prison in an hour, but Falke persuades him to an evening of delightful dissipation at the Villa Orlofsky, "where the young Russian prince lives, who is painting this little town red". It will be time enough for Eisenstein to give himself up in the morning. The Prince has asked Falke to bring some likely guests along, and nothing will do but that Gabriel shall take farewell of his unsuspecting wife, and slip off to the ball instead of to prison. A lot of amusing

[1] English version of the libretto by Alfred Kalisch.

by-play accompanies all this business, and the husband
finally tears himself away, leaving Rosalind in a paroxysm
of crocodile tears accompanied by much chromatic sobbing
of the violins.

Alfred, the tenor, immediately reappears, and proceeds
to regale himself with the wines and sweets placed on the
table for Eisenstein, and moreover, to slip into the absentee's
comfortable dressing gown and smoking cap. He and
Rosalind are in the midst of a sharp but melodious altercation when Frank, the Governor of the Gaol, arrives to
give himself the pleasure of personally escorting the
dear lady's husband to prison. Rosalind, to save her
reputation, immediately rises to the situation and thrusts
Alfred into this rôle. To reassure the somewhat dubious
Frank she sings

> "Does not what you see and hear
> Make the situation clear?
> The hour so late,
> So intimate,
> How like a husband this!
> His look of gloom,
> His loose costume,
> Can only mean connubial bliss!"

The Governor is persuaded as to the gentleman's identity,
and finally leads Alfred away after he and the captive and
Rosalind have given the famous song about the "schönes
grosses Vogelhaus"—the "birdcage airy, bright, and large"—
in which, as far as the lady knows, both her husband and her
lover will now be "sitting" for a week. She herself sinks
fainting into an armchair, and the curtain falls on the first
act.

The second act consists of the famous and spirited ballroom scene—the scene into which Strauss worked all his
experiences of Paris and Pavlovsk. A very rich young man,

bored with life much after the approved style of to-day, gives a ball on the one condition that nobody else should be, for one second, bored. There isn't much likelihood of Strauss letting them be! Never was such a merry evening staged before. A number of theatrical ladies are among the guests, including Molly, a sister of Frau Eisenstein's maid, Adèle. The sick aunt whom Adèle had vainly requested permission to visit, was, in reality, at this ball. Rosalind relented towards Adèle at the end of the first act, so the maid now appears, ravishingly dressed in one of her mistress's gowns, and is taken for an actress. Molly, it surprises her to learn, was not the sender of the tempting invitation which had prompted her to this escapade. Someone seems to have been playing jokes. . . .

Orlofsky, the host, saunters in with Dr. Falke from the garden, and sings what Decsey inimitably calls "ein couplet vom biographischen Farbenschimmer"—"in my eighteen years, Doctor, I have lived through forty. . . ."

Falke promises him amusement enough for to-night, at least, having prepared a little dramatic joke for the occasion. "What is the name of the piece?" demands the Prince, and Falke replies "The Bat's Revenge!"

Adèle and Molly present themselves. Falke congratulates himself, as he catches sight of the former, that his letter had its effect. His play begins. He lets the Prince into the joke, and tells him "this Olga is really the lady's maid to our hero's wife."

At that moment Eisenstein, the hero or dupe, himself appears as "Monsieur le Marquis de Renard" and is duly presented to Orlofsky, who invites him to wine, and treats him to the immortal polka in E major, "Bei uns ist das so Sitte", otherwise "Chacun à son goût", while Falke, smitten with another bright idea, dashes off an urgent note of invitation to Rosalind left alone in the Eisenstein apartment. He suggests she shall come as an Hungarian Countess incognito, and—masked!

Molly and Adèle reappear from the cardroom, where they have been losing money gaily for the Prince, and Eisenstein is immensely taken aback at recognising his wife's maid. A great fuss arises over this, as Adèle—"Mdlle. Olga"— pretends to be vastly affronted. Eisenstein can only attempt to make his blunder good by being specially polite to her for the next half-hour. The general amusement and indignation are only just allayed as a fresh guest is announced, Monsieur le Chevalier de Chagrin, none other than Frank, the Governor of the Prison. The two supposed Frenchmen, the Chevalier and the Marquis, are introduced to each other, and skate on the thin ice of wholly inadequate French for a moment, without either having the least idea who the other really is, while Falke and Orlofsky chuckle together over the thickening of the former's plot—whatever it may be.

The supper is delayed on account of a fair guest, not yet arrived, "on whose behalf", Falke sings, "I request the discretion of all the company." It seems she is married to a man so jealous that she cannot frequent society like this without a mask.

Everybody's interest is excited. More fun goes on until Rosalind finally appears. Eisenstein and Adèle retreat to flirt in the garden. Falke receives the late comer and assures her that what he wrote to bring her here was true. She could now take stock of matters for herself. "A look into the garden," he says drawing her up stage, "will convince you. There you can see how your husband is serving his sentence."

Rosalind catches sight of her husband with a laughing lady on his arm—and the laughing lady is Adèle! She has only a second to adjust her mask before Eisenstein and

Frank appear, arm in arm, in the highest and gayest of spirits. She is amazed to see him in the Governor's company thus, and calling himself a Marquis into the bargain! Only when Falke draws their attention to the lady does their boisterousness resolve into the *empressement* suitable to this new introduction. This, then, is the beautiful and mysterious Hungarian Countess for whom they have all been waiting!

Rosalind, inwardly vowing vengeance upon him, falls into merry conversation with the delighted Eisenstein, and feigns to be interested in a little repeater watch he presently shows her. There is a lot of amusing "business" about this watch. Eisenstein has often boasted of the conquests he has achieved by means of it, and if Rosalind can only get hold of it now, a thing no fair one has hitherto achieved, she will be able to turn the tables finely on him in due course. Naturally she succeeds, to Eisenstein's highly melodious indignation, and the general laughter at his discomfiture dissolves as the whole company fall to dancing. It is here that Strauss introduces his glorious Hungarian Csardas.

At the end of it Orlofsky demands the story of "The Bat" from Eisenstein.

"We were both living in a small town not far from here," laughs Eisenstein, "Falke had already started in practice but I was still a bachelor. At a country house not far from our town there was a fancy dress ball to which we were invited. I went as a butterfly and the Doctor as a bat, tightly sewn up in a thick brown skin, long claws, broad wings, and a yellow beak. To cut a long story short, when morning came he had had more than was good for him, and as we drove home through the woods, the coachman and I lifted him out, and very gently and tenderly placed him in the shade of a spreading tree and left him there all unconscious of his fate. When he awoke there was no help for it. In broad daylight he had to walk home through

the town to the great joy of all the street arabs. After that
he was known in all the district as 'Dr. Bat.'"

The story is received with gusto, and then the cry is
"To supper, to supper!" Orlofsky sings the first verse of the
champagne song.

> "Good wine to youth restores us,
> > Tra la la!
> It kills the thoughts that bore us,
> > Tra la la!
> Though power be their chief pleasure,
> Vain glory though they treasure,
> E'en kings find relaxation
> In rational potation.
> Then all your voices raise
> The King of Wines to praise!"

Bubbling figures for violin and viola give the note for the
famous champagne chorus:

> "His sovereignty we all acclaim!
> In all the world supreme his fame;
> King Fizz the First, King Fizz the First
> Shall be his name!"

Eisenstein and Adèle follow up this lead, and then comes
Falke's inspired suggestion

> "So let us a great confraternity found
> Be brothers and sisters all around."

The fun of these "beschwipsten Himmelfahrten"[1] waxes
ever faster and more furious. They dance and drink, and
the hours fly, and a general set is made at Rosalind to induce
her to unmask. Eisenstein has long abandoned Adèle and
given himself up to the passionate pursuit of the fair
incognita—his wife. She persists in her refusal to reveal

---

[1] Tipsy revellers bound for paradise, but nothing is half so funny as
the original.

herself. At length the clock strikes six in the morning, whereupon Frank has to hurry away to his official duties, and Eisenstein must rush off to give himself up at the prison. The curtain comes down on Act II with the chorus right heartily applauding the finest time of their lives.

Act III introduces Frosch, the tipsy Prison Warder, an immortal figure of fun.

The opening scene of Act III is a veritable psychological study in music of the condition known as "the morning after the night before", drawn from Strauss' personal experience. A gentleman comes staggering into his office, "cylinder" hat tilted over his eyes, and coat oddly buttoned. "The muted violins yawn . . . the violas betray a certain feverishness . . . the bassoons are oddly reminiscent." Ah! it is the Prison Governor, Frank! Previously the Frank motif had rung out trumpet clear, sober as the day. Now, however, it has undergone a change. The music parodies itself and Frank. As the reveller sinks into his chair and falls asleep, the double bass snores too.

No more striking contrast than this could have been found to the fun fast and furious of the preceding scene. Strauss was very undecided whether or not to emphasise it—or even to retain it. Marie Geistinger implored him, at rehearsal, to cut the whole thing out, but Genée, with a better appreciation of the sheer artistry of the portrayal, over-persuaded him again, and Frank's "business" remained. The whole scene is inimitably funny.

The ladies who have arrived are Adèle and her sister Molly, and with them begin the series of revelations and explanations and confessions, with which the impersonations and mystifications and complications of the ball at Prince Orlofsky's are now to be cleared up.

Adèle declared she is no actress but maid to Frau von

Eisenstein. She has done with service from now on, and Molly wants Frank to help her sister to go on the stage. They are in the midst of pressing this suggestion upon him when the bell goes again, and Frank, taking a look through the window, discovers the Marquis de Renard! Frosch is hurriedly ordered to get rid of the girls—any-where—anyhow. He escorts them to the cells and locks them up.

Eisenstein and Frank, the Marquis and the Chevalier, are mutually astounded to find each other here. More explanations follow. Eisenstein will not believe that the Chevalier is the Governor of the Gaol, until the latter, summoning Frosch once more, orders him to arrest the Marquis. Whereupon the latter reveals his own identity and another laughable tangle ensues.

Frank excuses himself to Eisenstein, struck dumb with consternation and astonishment, and hurries out followed by the Warder.

Then Frosch returns ushering in Blind, the lawyer, for whom the supposed Eisenstein (Alfred) has sent.

"What's he talking about?" asks Blind, of Eisenstein, "How can he go and fetch Eisenstein? You're here!"

"I'm not only here, but also there," answers the confused and stricken husband. Then in a flash, "I want your coat, your wig, your spectacles, your papers, Hurry up!"

He bundles Blind out of the room, and changes clothes and places with him. Frosch ushers Alfred in, still clad in dressing gown and smoking cap, and is amazed not to find the lawyer where he left him, in the waiting-room. Rosalind appears. There is a lot of fun, and at length Eisenstein, disguised as Blind, the lawyer, comes upon the supposedly guilty pair.

Alfred and Rosalind exculpate themselves without being

able to satisfy this curious sort of lawyer. At length Eisenstein reveals himself and sings the semi-comic semi-tragic

> "Ja, ich bin's, den Ihr betrogen,"
> "Yes, it is I, whom you have deceived"

which Rosalind echoes, equally vehemently, in her turn.

The musical altercation goes on, till Rosalind springs the watch on Eisenstein. If he was the Marquis, she was the Hungarian! And Alfred cries "So you are Herr von Eisenstein?" to which Gabriel replies, now beaming,

"Yes, I am Eisenstein. The proud possessor of this lovely lady and that dressing gown."

Reconciliation brings the comedy of errors 'twixt husband and wife to a happy close, and Alfred is rejoiced that the rightful culprit should be ready to take his place in the cell "which I have kept warm for him".

Adèle and Molly, who have been making a frightful fuss in cell 13, are now released by the Governor, and still more explanations are cut short by Falke owning up that the whole thing was a joke devised by him to get his own back on Eisenstein. Everything ends in a fresh outburst of hilarity and fun. Adèle comes off extremely well. The cost of having her undoubted talents trained for the stage will be borne not by Frank but by the lordly Orlofsky, who unaccountably but quite necessarily turns up in this extraordinary prison for the final dances and choruses, and explains his gesture,

> "Chacun à son goût!"

So much for the story of "Die Fledermaus". "I do not know," says Decsey, "whether Strauss was qualified to write opera. I only know that he did a lot of excellent work, and composed one thing which will live."

It went into rehearsal immediately upon completion and was produced at the Theater-an-der-Wien on the 5th of April, 1874. The first night was a brilliant success, but again there were not wanting a number of critics to find fault with the music. A strange legend, indeed, was to grow up that it was not wholly original, that Strauss had derived a good deal of it from the mass of manuscripts left behind by Josef. Decsey makes short work of this contention, and shows by a fine musical scrutiny of the work, how it could only have emanated from the man of whose musical genius alone it is demonstrably the product. Dr. Hanslick would have the Viennese composer observe that any comparison instituted between himself and Offenbach could only redound to the latter's enhanced prestige.

In spite of its warm reception by the opera-going public the piece was withdrawn after sixteen performances. The Theatre was not doing well financially, the Manager wanted to overhaul his repertory, and the stage was required for Madame Patti.

Strauss made little of what might be described as the mere *Succès d'estime*, achieved by his "Bat". He applied Alfred's philosophy to himself.

> "Glücklich ist wer vergisst
> Was nicht mehr zu ändern ist."

> "He is happy who forgets
> What can no longer be altered."

The disappointment, however, was only apparent, and not at all real. And it was only temporary.

Johann received a call to Italy, and left Vienna for a highly successful tour as far as Rome with the Elberfeld Orchestra. The score of his Operetta was buried in the "Opera's cemetery," i.e. the bottommost drawer of the

Theatre Director's desk in Vienna, and everyone instantly forgot it.

But in Berlin the work met with a very different fate. The public went mad over it. Every evening the house was sold out; five or six of the outstanding melodies in the piece were encored insatiably. The critics exhausted superlatives in belauding it. When this sort of news reached Vienna, Director Steiner was thoroughly nonplussed. "What in the world do those Berliners mean?" he puzzled. "Text and music are all right, but the thing doesn't draw! I've laid out no end on it, and got practically nothing in return. One evening of Patti brought in more than six of the 'Fledermaus'. And yet it's such a hit in Berlin! Perhaps I'd better give it another try."

Fortunately he acted on these second thoughts, and was presently justified by the result. Vienna gradually woke up to "Die Fledermaus". The Theater-an-der-Wien found itself packed out now whenever the Operetta was billed. It was recognised as a masterpiece. The Director could not congratulate himself enough, and revelled in the glory of having "discovered" the new operatic composer.

In Hamburg it soon reached its 200th performance, and in Paris it had a great success—in somewhat altered guise —and was added to the repertory of the Renaissance Theatre. Everybody there delighted in it except Offenbach, who, as an old man now crippled with the gout, cared for nothing but his work on the "Tales of Hoffmann". "Fledermaus" had come to stay. Nothing, to-day, can stale the sheer beauty, the tunefulness, the never-to-be-hackneyed themes, one after another, of the immortal Overture. The Radio may give it to us on all its programmes as many days in the week as it likes, and it catches us away at once into a world all charm, all laughter. There is the Tritsch-Tratsch Polka, The Laughing Song, the Czardas, the jodel-derived hymn to the champagne, the waltzes, the duets, and all the rest of it! 'Fledermaus, said Mr. Holbrook, Manager of Sadler's Wells, "definitely ranks amongst the most popular works in our repertoire"—and that, to-day, sixty-five years after that hectic bout of composition in Hietzinger Villa, at Vienna.

CHAPTER XVI

NO GILBERT FOR HIS SULLIVAN, '78

JOHANN STRAUSS had reached the zenith of success —this man, who only four decades before, started where his father left off. The grandson of the poor Gastwirt, of the Leopoldstadt, who had committed suicide, now set the fashions in Vienna. Johann was rich. He could ride, dine, drive, dress and live in the smartest style. He was presently to buy a charming country retreat for himself at Ischl, in Upper Austria, not far from Salzburg (where Brahms was to visit him), and also a "Palais" in the Igelgasse, in Vienna. He had bought up some property in the city, and caused some new houses to be built there after extensive demolitions had been carried out. He bought a place, "Gut Schönau", near Leobersdorf, where his gardeners grew asparagus, and he himself could play the Grand Seigneur, strolling about in a violet silk dressing-gown between the intervals of composition.

He was always and for ever writing. He had, in fact, to do himself violence to check or resist the incessant flow of musical ideas which beset him. They interrupted his recreations, cards, or billiards, and drove him away to jot them down. Not that he needed piano or violin in order to seize a melody. He just pounced for anything handy to write on, a scrap of note paper, a handkerchief, his own shirt cuffs, a hundred pound bank note, or even the very sheets of the bed in which his wife lay quietly sleeping by his side! It is said that Frau Jetty saved the "Beautiful Blue Danube" itself from being sent to the wash! She noticed some musical notes on one of her husband's cuffs, just in time.

Strauss was an inspirational composer, like his father. He would, indeed, rewrite a couplet or a passage twice or a dozen times before it entirely pleased him, but he cared not at all for the elaboration of his spontaneous work. He left its counterpoint and "arrangement" to others. Perhaps two dozen expert musicians are to be numbered among those who have taken the Strauss themes and further developed them. How much unacknowledged influence his works may have had upon other writers' compositions is hardly to be estimated. "Nor," says Decsey, "can an idea be lightly formed of what sort of a genius would have resulted, had nature united the immense musical culture of a Brahms with the inexhaustible inspiration of a Strauss in one and the same person!"

In the spring of the "Fledermaus" year, as has been said, Johann went to Italy with the orchestra which he had conducted during the International Exhibition.

Diplomatic relations, of course, had been resumed between Italy and Austria, after the war in 1866, but the Italians could not forget too quickly all they had suffered in the past from Austrian oppression, and the name of Radetzky was still cordially hated throughout the country. Franz Josef, however, had taken advantage of the Exhibition to send a specially courteous invitation to the King of Italy, begging him to visit Vienna, and Victor Emmanuel had hastened to accept it. This gesture, on both sides, had made towards international reconciliation, but it is not too much to say that Johann's tour did a great deal more to this end, and did it better! After Johann nothing but Viennese music was played, danced, sung and hummed in Italy, as years before nothing but Italian music had been heard in Vienna. Prince, Count, gondolier and beggar alike fell victims to the

N

music of Strauss. The bitterest irredentist had nothing to say against this sort of Austrian conquest.

In Italy he composed "Where the lemon trees bloom" (Wo die Zitronen blüh'n) one of his most poetic waltzes, which so delighted Genée that he wrote some words for it and turned it into a song. The Geistinger gave it for the first time in public.

Then, next year, when the Emperor Franz Josef expressed a desire to return the King of Italy's visit, all Venice came out to meet the two monarchs with the most cordial demonstrations of goodwill. The two countries were reconciled and the hostility of generations was laid aside. The day had come (and its coming had been hastened by Strauss), which the great Venetian patriot, Daniel Manin, foretold in 1847 when "Italy, reconstituted as a nation, will be the first friend of Austria."

Strange, what an echo these far-off things seem, at times, to have to-day!

Strauss' next Operetta, produced in February, 1875, was a curious work called "Cagliostro in Wien". The librettist only just succeeded in not bringing the thing off. He had hit on a promising theme and period which offered Strauss just what he was looking for, something national, Austrian, Viennese. This was the visit of Cagliostro to the Danubian capital at the time it was celebrating the centenary of its deliverance from the Turks in 1684. The Italian adventurer and charlatan lays himself out to fool the naïve Viennese to the top of their bent. He has a laboratory, and professes the art of transmuting the common metals into gold. His beautiful young wife, Lorenza Feliciani, comes into the play, and gives occasion for some musical love-making.

The first Act gave Johann immense scope. It staged a Viennese festival at the end of the eighteenth century, in

By courtesy of the Director of the Historical Collections of the City of Vienna.

THE THEATER-AN-DER-WIEN.

the true rococo period. The Master took his gayest, brightest palette to paint this scene, and achieved a brilliant picture. The weaker the text became as the very poor story proceeded, the more lavishly Strauss laid on his musical colours. But the liveliest music is badly handicapped when the plot ceases to interest the audience.

The play, as a play, was so feeble that "Cagliostro" achieved but a questionable success. Two things alone redeemed it, the Strauss music and Alexander Girardi.

Girardi was a marvel. This young actor, originally a locksmith's journeyman from Graz, now twenty-five years old, possessed a voice, neither tenor nor baritone, but glorious, flexible and extraordinarily true. It had never been trained, nor could Girardi read music! But his ear was perfect, and his memory too. Once having heard a song, he could repeat it faultlessly. The producers of the Operetta, one and all, had work enough to train this singer for the title rôle, but once Girardi mastered it, largely thanks to the indefatigable Strauss, his delightful performance fully recompensed their efforts. Girardi did all that could be done to infuse life into the sticks that did duty for characters in this piece. He became the darling of the theatre-going public, and in future no librettist or composer in Vienna set pen to paper without having him in view.

Good fun as "Fledermaus" was, it cannot be claimed for Strauss' most successful operetta that the libretto was worth one note of the music. Strauss never found a libretto worthy of his composer's pen. It is really a sad thing that this was so. For there must have been *somebody* in that galaxy of writers for the lighter stage at that period, both at home and abroad, who could have offered something far worthier of him than he ever got.

The critics have often reproached him with lack of theatrical instinct in this matter, both rightly and wrongly.

It is easier to find fault with a poor libretto than to hit upon a good one. Even Jetty's advice was not always to be relied upon. Occasionally she let a good thing slip, and voted for the second best. The most experienced people can go astray over this. No one knows, in the publishing world, why a best seller *is* a best seller, and no one knows in the theatrical world whether a thing will catch on. What reads like the best of fun in the text may fall inexplicably flat on the stage. Attractive characters, in the book, may fail to get any charm across the footlights, and stupidities which should obviously be blue pencilled, bring down the house!

Something, however, must be ascribed to the make of man that Strauss was—to his own personality, strange admixture of so many strains. He lived out of touch with the better literary circles in Vienna, and cared less for poetic than for more mundane talents in those who collaborated with him. It often happened, when he invited men of outstanding parts to his house, that, shocking to relate, this one used a knife to his peas, or the other failed to turn up in evening dress! He found fault with them for some irrelevant triviality,—Strauss, the grandson of the Bierwirt, yet in whom perhaps ran some drop of proud and finicky Spanish blood! It was his loss that he possessed no wide outlook on things or the times, but this was the fault of his class and contemporaries quite as much as his own.

Again, Strauss could scarcely escape the penalties of his profession. The composer of an Operetta is given over to the "Shylock instinct" of his producers, his competitors, and his own ambition. He is a veritable slave to the theatrical manager's demand for novelty.

Whatever the cause of it may have been, the fact remains that Strauss was unlucky in his choice of librettos. Other men succeeded, with the very thing he may have turned

down, irresolute and doubtful, in favour of a "dud" like
"Prince Methuselah!"

Herr Franz von Jauner, the Director of the Karl Theater,
had managed to entice Johann away from the Theater-an-
der-Wien by offering him something written specially for
him in the Parisian manner.

The piece was produced in January, 1877. It was a failure.
Strauss may have been a god and an idol in Vienna, but
this is by no means to say that his public accepted anything
from him merely because he wrote it. Strauss' public ever
remained exacting to the last degree, all the more so perhaps
just because he was the King. This is real musical discrimina-
tion. Less perceptive critics will hail anything coming from
a master's pen as a masterpiece. Not so the Viennese.
Strauss' "Methuselah" bored his audience, and filled his
fans with concern.

He was accustomed to say that he wrote as much for the
gallery as for the stalls, and that, inasmuch as the "gods"
at that time were not often possessed of technical musical
education, and still less of a piano, their memory was all
they could fall back upon for their music. Hence the melodies
he wrote must be the melodies the people in the gallery
could take away with them and make their own. The
"May Waltz", and two or three other characteristic Strauss
hits, were all the gods could take home from "Methuselah".
The story fell flat, and so damned a score in itself by no
means unworthy of the writer. "Methuselah" fell flat,
and the composer went off on tour again after its sixth
performance.

He went to Leipzig, Hamburg, Dresden, Baden-Baden and
Berlin. He gave a series of immediately successful concerts
at the Kroll Opera House, and was much admired personally.

Later he went to Paris, where he felt himself entirely at
home—he spoke French well—to conduct a series of magnifi-

cent balls in co-operation with Olivier Métra. Gone were
Napoleon and Eugénie, but Parisian society could still be
gay under the Third Republic. Métra had arisen in the
French metropolis, a Parisian Strauss, and although the
original "import from Vienna" now set the fashion even
in gloves and ties and hats, Métra's orchestra decided it was
not compatible with their national honour to divide allegiance
between the two great men. "Hasn't Strauss had enough
French adulation?" they demanded. And some of the
newspapers exacerbated susceptibilities still more, by
reporting that the Viennese master had spoken slightingly
of French music. Quite a pretty fuss got up. Strauss became
fiery in his turn, and could scarcely be dissuaded from tearing
up his contract and turning his back on Paris then and
there. He was convinced they meant to hiss him on his next
appearance in public at a great masquerade in the Opera
house, but the Director implored him to pay no attention
to gossip and the gutter press. Strauss repelled the impu-
tation that he wished to compete with Métra in any way,
and the Director went to the utmost extremes of Gallic
vehemence to assure him that he was as beloved of the
general Parisian public as ever. The whole thing was as
hectic as it is funny in retrospect. Immense success, on
the evening in question, justified everybody, Métra, Strauss,
and the Director. And Strauss took occasion before leaving
Paris to make a handsome donation to the funds of a Parisian
musical organisation, which adroit gesture was gracefully
received, so that everything ended in smiles and mutual
compliments. A final distinction, greatly appreciated by
its recipient, was Strauss' investiture by the President of the
Republic with the quite inevitable cross of the Légion
d'Honneur.

He returned home with his cup of success in life so riotously
brimful and running over, that the fate which had filled it,

impish and uncertain as Viennese popularity itself, now
thought it fun to do some ruthless spilling. . . .

After sixteen years of happy married life with her Johann,
Frau Jetty was at length to realise that it is an unfortunate
thing for a woman to be ten years older than her husband,
and this especially in such a case as theirs. Strauss was at
the zenith of a glamorous career, and still a comparatively
young man. He was the darling of international society,
and the *beau idéal* of the women of a dozen capitals. And
he had never pretended to be insusceptible to feminine charms
or blandishments. If there was little of the roué about
Strauss, there was still less of the moralist.

Jetty, on the other hand, was in middle life. Her day was
past and over. The St. Martin's summer, that had been her
marriage, broke up into autumnal gales. Johann gave her
much occasion for heartache and jealousy. She did what she
could with the aid of dress and cosmetics to hold him,
but he absented himself from home more and more, spent
his leisure abroad, and under the thinnest of pretexts
frequented the society at Dommayer's without his wife.

His regular appearance of an evening in the Casino or the
coffee house puzzled his friends, who knew how much his
own place meant to him.

The shrewd, the sympathetic, or the malicious might
detect that all was not as it should be with Strauss, under
his assumption of ease and gaiety. Something was inhibiting
his work, something was souring his life. . . .

The fault by no means lay wholly at his own door. Quarrels
had arisen in the Hietzinger Villa, and scenes took place, at
once dreadful and sordid, in which it would have been hard
to tell who was most to be pitied, the husband or the wife.
Strauss and Jetty had come to a pass in their lives which
offered material, handled by a master, for serious and tragic
opera. He, perhaps, was breaking the heart of a faulty

woman, but at least of a true and devoted wife, who as "secretary, diplomatist, finance minister, producer, impresario" had steered him from success to success, and to professional heights he might not have attained without her.

But the fate which now intervened to spill his cup, also flung open a door in Jetty's past to reveal things out of the gay days of her youth in the theatre, long forgotten, long buried, long forgiven. . . .

The pity was Johann hadn't known. His mother's restiveness at the time of his engagement to Jetty had seemed to him mere prejudice. But maternal instinct is not often at fault.

A son turned up—a son of whose existence Jetty's husband had been kept in total ignorance. He demanded money from his mother, and that in no niggardly measure. The poor thing gave him all she could afford, but the man, indecent enough to bank on the fact of her being the wife of a very successful celebrity, attempted further demands on Strauss. Johann indignantly refused him a stiver, whereupon Jetty herself became resentful. The state of affairs in the Hietzinger Villa went from bad to worse. Husband and wife were practically parted. If ever they were seen together now, it was only for the sake of appearances.

Strauss came back from Paris in March and tried to work. It was springtime again. The trees in the garden of the Villa, and in the great park of Schönbrunn beyond, were bursting into leaf and blossom. The master's study was flooded with sunlight, but it was easier for him, just now, to spend his time over the architect's plans for his new palace in the Igelgasse—nearer the Theatre—than to compose. The living-rooms, and his work-rooms, music-room, studio and so forth, were to be upon the ground floor; the drawing-rooms and reception-rooms above, with servant's quarters on the third storey. There were to be stables, a well laid out garden with flowers, and glasshouses. The walls were already rising. Strauss discussed the progress and the details of his house with his friends at Dommayer's, instead of libretti with Genée and Steiner.

The end of an intolerable situation came suddenly. He returned home from the Casino one evening to find his whole household in a state of distress and alarm. Frau Jetty had had a stroke! Strauss hastened to her room and found her unconscious. Doctors, of course, were hastily summoned, and did all they could, but in vain. It seems she had received a letter which had terribly upset her, and this was the result. Johann knew only too well from whom it had come. . . .

Nothing could help her now. Jetty lay, broken and suffering, for some days, and then quietly died, April 7, 1878.

It was a great blow to Strauss. Anger dropped away from him. Mute at the bedside, he had only to be grateful to that still, white, sleeping form for the love it had shown him. As he took the waxen fingers in his hand to imprint a farewell kiss upon them, he was suddenly seized by the morbid horror of death which had always characterised him. He turned and fled from the room. He fled from the house. He could not tolerate the idea of spending the night in it, under the same roof as a corpse! He gave what orders were necessary, and hurried away to his sisters, at the old Hirschenhaus. Both women were dreadfully upset by the news, and scandalised to realise that Johann intended leaving the city at once. The brother Edouard was sent for and charged with the whole of the funeral arrangements.

All three together could not prevail upon the distraught, temperamental man to see reason or common decency in this matter. His horror of the Kirchof and of everything to do with death was too ingrained, and this sudden passing of a wife from whom he had become estranged rather emphasised it than the reverse. Johann caught the night express from Vienna and fled, without telling anyone of his destination, or caring in the least what Vienna made of his extraordinary absence at the funeral.

Jetty was laid to rest in due course, and was sincerely mourned by a large circle of friends, who loved and respected her. Few people had known much of the strife which had crept in between husband and wife and estranged them at the last. For the Viennese public she remained the woman who had been the valued helpmate of their beloved Johann Strauss. R.I.P.

CHAPTER XVII

CHANGE OF KEY: '83

WHAT happened next was so ridiculous, so ill-considered, so precipitate, that it serves to show the utter disorientation Strauss had suffered, first from the recent troubles in his domestic life, and secondly from the shock of Jetty's sudden and pitiful death.

He married again within a few weeks! Not one of the various ladies of whom poor Jetty may have had real or imaginary cause to be jealous, but a girl hitherto a stranger to him. Fräulein Angelika Diettrich, from Cologne, was certainly the most disastrous libretto to which the master could devote his energies. Here, again, he showed no perspicacity, no instinct for intrinsic worth. . . .

After Jetty's death Johann could not bear the empty house in the Hietzingerstrasse, nor could he make up his mind to move into the big place in the Igelgasse. So he went for a time to live in the Hotel Victoria.

He fell into a state of sheer joylessness and utter indecision. He found himself beset by daily cares and worries, by things to which he had never hitherto given a thought, and with which he could not cope. He craved the peace and order Jetty had assured to his life, and with every day that went by he missed her more, and realised and mourned her loss the deeper.

It happened at this juncture that a Herr Proch, Director of Music to the Court, was accustomed to take his evening glass of beer, together with a circle of friends and professional colleagues, in the leafy gardens of the Hotel

Victoria. Naturally Strauss was to be found there, too. One evening Proch mentioned that a young singer from Cologne, a young actress who had already appeared in Linz, had come to him for a further course of study. He would be glad of Strauss' opinion on her voice.

This was Angelika Diettrich, or Lily as she preferred to be called, a girl whose "Venetian" fairness and singular beauty had more to do than her singing with the warm praise the recently widowed Master instantly accorded her. Strauss, dazzled by a vision which intrigued his senses no less than his eyes, suffered a sudden and irrational reaction. He fell violently in love! Lily caught him on the rebound from Jetty. Her May was such a contrast to the weeping October through which he had lived of late.

Johann Strauss is not the only example on record of a widower plunging into a marriage which is an act of precipitate and obvious folly, almost before a good wife is cold in her grave. In his case it would be a poor student of humanity indeed who failed to understand it. All Vienna laughed, but all sensible Vienna also shook a more than doubtful head. The humorous papers quoted from his own Operetta, "Happy he who forgets——", but Lily was proud to find herself mistress in the Igelgasse, and Johann, at fifty-three, thought it a glorious indication of his irresistibility to be seen in public with such a bride hanging on his arm. . . . Everyone turned to stare at the new Frau Strauss with unfeigned admiration.

The newly married pair spent their honeymoon at Schönau. Strauss had chosen a truly idyllic spot for his country home some hours distant by rail from the capital. The house was princely, set among broad terraces, in a park-like garden with avenues of trees and wide-spread parterres. The composer took a dilettante's interest in rose grafting and asparagus culture, but even so he enjoyed

the excuse of a wet day in the country, to shut himself
up in his study and write music. He began a new operetta
at Schönau in the midst of his honeymoon. But the score
of the "Blindekuh" (Blind Cow) would sufficiently reveal
much to a psychoanalist about the whole of this curious
passage in his life. The "Blind Cow" was Johann's one
outstanding failure.

In the first place, he was less qualified than usual to
bring anything like clear-headedness and good judgment
to bear upon his choice of a libretto. In the second, he now
possessed no sound, experienced adviser in his wife. In
the third, the Strauss music for this work was—with the
exception of a few numbers—not quite worthy of him.

The piece (produced at the Theater-an-der-Wien, 18th
December, 1878), was based upon a comedy by Rudolf
Kneifel, and turned upon the complications of a marriage
and a will in middle-class society. The libretto was so excessively poor that it practically killed even the Strauss music.

Next came the "Spitzentuch" (the Queen's Lace Handkerchief) in which the Master largely regained his form.

The story behind this operetta is interesting. A few weeks
after the failure of Strauss' "Blindekuh", Suppé reaped the
big success of his life with "Boccaccio", at the Karltheater.
In May he went with the opera to Pressburg, and asked the
Director of the theatre there, Heinrich Bohrmann, himself
a successful dramatist, to write something new for him.
Bohrmann consented, and wrote a witty piece called "The
Queen's Lace Handkerchief", but when he arrived in Vienna
with the sketch of it, a few weeks later, he found Suppé
already at work again on something else. So he offered it
to Strauss, who jumped at it. In this roundabout way
Suppé's success redounded to another success for Johann.

The "Spitzentuch" was produced on the 1st of October,
1880, in the Theater-an-der-Wien, and proved to be the

most lucrative show put on there for six years. The Fürst-
theater in the Prater staged an amusing Parody "Das
Schnupftuch des Kongis" (The King's wet Handkerchief)
with music *after* Johann Strauss. Girardi was heard to
perfection in the "Spitzentuch", and covered himself and
composer with fresh laurels.

The story had it that once upon a time a Portuguese
Queen wrote on her handkerchief "A Queen loves you although
you are no King." The words referred to her husband who
was not yet King, inasmuch as he had not yet attained his
majority. The country was under the control of the Premier.
Somehow or other Cervantes contrives that the royal minor,
instead of reading some innocuous speech from the throne,
should officially declare himself of age. The Premier revenges
himself by suggesting that the declaration on the Queen's
handkerchief referred to the Spanish poet. Whereupon
jealousies and dense misunderstandings arise, and the
usual complications follow. Cervantes is banished to the
country. Finally, however, as the Padron of a Posada, he
brings the estranged royal pair happily together again,
and they have a magnificent repast, which has become
one of the most famous dramatic and musical guzzles ever
staged. The well-known Truffles duet belongs to the
"Spitzentuch", and is one of the gems of its greedy text.

"Der Lustige Krieg", (The Merry War) the next and
eighth in the rapid series of Strauss' operettas, was also
partially written at Schönau. (Produced in November '81.)

[1] "Ach, von Zweifeln werd ich schon geplagt,
   Mir bangt vor dieser Ehe Glück,
   Doch leider hab' Ich Ja gesagt,
   Ich kann nicht mehr zurück.
                Violetta in the "Lustiger Krieg".

[1] "Ah, I am already very doubtful as to this marriage, and afraid it
will not turn out happily, but unfortunately I have said yes to it, and
cannot go back on my word."

Strauss was not a happy man when he sat down to write
"Der Lustige Krieg". He was already aware that his second
venture into matrimony was a failure. But he never obtruded
his private griefs into his work. His inmost spirit was
unquenchable.

If Jetty had ever wished to be revenged on Johann,
which we can be sure she never did—what good wife ever
does?—the completely heartless young beauty from Cologne
was quite equal to the task.

Lily was bored with her celebrity. Bored with Schönau.
Bored at having to take music in earnest. She had been
flattered, and greedy, and ambitious. But she was far too
young to rest contented with position and wealth and
even with love, if youth were not included. She failed
Strauss almost from the beginning. She began to taunt
him about his age. Johann, the adored of European femin-
inity, found himself scorned and flouted in his own house
by the most delectable specimen of it he had yet encountered!
Johann, far from being irresistible, was repulsed. Johann,
previously the petted husband of a highly appreciative
wife, was now become a lamentable figure of French comedy.

They returned eventually to Vienna, and Strauss went
on with his work. But he was very unhappy. For the first
time in adult life he came face to face with the cruelty that
only utterly selfish youth can betray. Lily cared nothing
for his art, because he was "old", and nothing for his fame,
and for the esteem in which Vienna held him, for the same
flimsy reason. She imagined her life with him would have
been considerably gayer. She constantly upbraided him with
having cajoled her into a marriage which disappointed her.

So Strauss took refuge in his study and composed another
operetta. Zell and Genée wrote the text of "The Merry War",
round a subject which the sheer genius of Girardi, as well
as that of the composer, lifted to the rank of acknowledged

comic opera. In this bloodless "War", mostly waged by ladies, the prima donna Violetta is to marry the Duke of Nimburg, who is at loggerheads with the Genoese. One of the Genoese Generals, Umberto, pretends to be a representative of the Duke's, sent to marry her by proxy, but as it turns out he marries her himself. A Dutch bulb merchant, Groot, comes into the piece and impersonates the Duke. The whole thing is witty and has been favourably compared with Suppé's "Boccaccio".

It was given in the Theater-an-der-Wien on the 25th of November, 1881, and was enthusiastically received. Strauss had been more than profuse with his accustomed melodiousness. Although the advance he had made in the handling of the orchestra and in the arrangement of the vocal parts, may have escaped the majority of the audience, it was quite equal to recognising a masterpiece in "The Merry War". Girardi, now one of the lions in Vienna, was not content with his rôle, unless Strauss would insert an outstanding solo specially for him. The Master was loathe to accede, but realising, as he did, how Girardi alone could be relied upon to redeem a performance at any one of its weaker points, and of what untold value his unique performance was, he finally agreed. He chose an exquisite theme for his inexhaustible treasury of musical notes and sketches, and wrote the "Naturwalzer". Girardi was very particular as to the words to be set to this melody. The number proved to be *the* great success of his life. It made him. If he ranked already among the Viennese lions, Strauss' leading tenor now became the idol, the oracle, the god of the Austrian light opera stage. Everything turned thenceforth on Girardi. The operetta, from this time forth, became first and foremost a vehicle for Girardi, and to this extent the type and style of Strauss' theatrical work underwent a change.

A fortnight after "Der Lustige Krieg" had been put on at the Theater-an-der-Wien, there was a terrible catastrophe. The Ring Theatre was burnt to the ground, just before a performance of the "Tales of Hoffmann" was about to begin. The curtain caught fire and a veritable holocaust resulted. Hundreds of people were burnt to death. It took whole weeks of work before all the charred bodies were recovered. The disaster plunged Vienna into mourning, and into a frenzy of righteous indignation against the authorities, to whose carelessness and inefficiency it had been largely due.

"The Merry War," at the Theater-an-der-Wien, was the only public entertainment which survived this calamity. It was not taken off, for Strauss could still tide the Viennese over anything! During one of the performances, an enthusiastic young musician in the stalls fell on his knees when the great quintette "Kommen und Geh'n" began, much as Linnaeus fell on his knees before the blossoming gorse!

Strauss had reconciled himself to the fact that his wife cared nothing for his music long before he could bear to realise that she had no use for him as a man. It was very bitter to him to live side by side with a woman who, far from caring for him in the least, made no secret of her boredom and indifference. . . .

It would be interesting to anticipate the playwright who is one day going to give us "Johann Strauss" on the stage.

Imagine a room in the house in the Igelgasse, luxuriously furnished with mirrors and consoles and hangings, after the style of the eighteen eighties. There might be a glorious red carpet with heavy upholstered furniture scattered over it in much studded blue rep. There would be a vast grand piano, and surely one or more of those queer three-seat settees which really do seem to have gone to limbo, with

o

a back like the arms of the Isle of Man. There would be fringed footstools and much too much of everything everywhere. . . .

Johann and Lily enter, returning from a drive in the Prater. The ill-concealed anger of a sorely vexed man breaks out. Throwing himself down in a chair,

"It is positively outrageous, Angelika," he exclaims; "you make me the laughing stock of the city! The way you dared to flirt with young von Hohenstein this afternoon under my very eyes was absolutely shameless."

Angelika tilts her chin and treats herself to another satisfying scrutiny of provoking new hat and mantle in the glass before she deigns to reply. Then she says lightly, "Jealous, Johann? Or do I steal your thunder?"

Fuming, he regards her with the bitterness of utter disillusionment in his dark, "malicious" glance.

"You disgrace me! You presume atrociously . . ."

"On what pray? My looks?"

He can scarcely admit it. Angelika is charming enough, outwardly, to turn more heads than those of the butterfly-like young men with whom she dances nightly into the small hours of the morning.

"On your position," he retorts, "as my wife."

She makes a contemptuous gesture, and would ring for her maid to come and disembarrass her of an elaborate toilette, if Johann does not interpose.

"You go too far," he says, and catches her dainty wrist, "I am at the end of my patience, Angelika——"

"Your patience!" she cries in sudden anger. "I wonder what you imagine that means? It is far more to the point to say that I am at the end of mine! Here am I tied to an old man, an old stick-at-home too, if he had his own way, who dares,—who *dares*, I say—to make a jealous fuss when I go into society. How can I help it if the men

admire me? And why shouldn't they? You don't suppose
I only dress for you?"

Strauss glares, bristles, struggles for words, then lets her
go free. She has, indeed, sorely pricked him. "Old." She
has called him "old"! That, of course, is the root of the
matter! He *is* old, compared with her blooming, selfish
arrogant youth.

Up to now Johann has always carried all before him.
He has even carried off this silly, crazy marriage. That is
because he has not realised the flight of time, and because
Jetty had been so much his senior. Angelika's savage little
outburst strikes the scales from his eyes. He drops her
wrist, turns away speechless, and presses out his cigar in
the ashtray.

His wife treats him to a glance of petulant surprise.

"It is you who presume," she retorts. "Did you really
imagine I was going to let myself be shut up alone with
you here, and never enjoy myself at all? When one is
young one must be gay——"

Truly the Waltz King's chickens are coming home to
roost! Strauss is the last man in the world to gainsay her
claim. But there is a "Misklang" in the music somewhere.
Try as he may to harmonise this passage in the symphony
of his own life, he now sees how fundamentally misconceived
the theme is. It escapes his technique as few unsatisfactory
resolutions have escaped it before. Nor can it be torn up
and cast aside like the rough draft of an operetta. . . .
Here the dance fails the dancers as no Strauss dance had
ever failed them yet. . . .

He had not known he was "old". He had not felt it.
There she stands, his flighty, pretty wife, provocative as
any woman (except a man's own wife) should be, and throws
it in his face that she had married an old man! It was as
if the fiddle bow had suddenly fallen from his hand.

Angelika flounces from the room, sensing something of her success. For the next day or so, perhaps, she will find it a little easier to pursue her special and private entertainments. Her husband will immerse himself once more in his work, and subside into ill-humour.

Poor Johann has little option.

We can imagine him staring after her, and then, left alone, asking himself presently if it wasn't his own fault for being such a fool as to marry this young creature . . .?

.   .   .   .   .

He felt, indeed, like a solitary, this man who could not do without a woman's affection, one for whom life had not much more, perhaps, in store. And Angelika was stranded too—alone. Alone indeed!

It was not likely that a young woman of Angelika's appearance and inclination would long remain alone. Strauss' absorption in his work would have caused a good deal of time to hang heavily on her hands, had she not known how to utilise it. She encouraged admirers . . . she delighted in the risk of flirtations . . . the state of affairs between her and her husband was not kept sedulously secret. In the course of four or five years Angelika gave up whatever attempts she may have made to tolerate existence as Frau Strauss. She eloped from Schönau one misty September evening, without leaving word or sign for her husband. The man with whom she ran away was none other than the Director Steiner, of the Theater-an-der-Wien, with whom Strauss had so long been on a footing of personal friendship as well of professional intimacy.

It was a painful "Coda" for Fate to have written at the end of the Lily episode. The whole affair was one of the few overcast passages in Strauss' life. Fortunately, resilient as his music, he survived it.

With the exception of "Die Fledermaus", it has scarcely been worth while to retail the stories of Strauss' operettas at any length. Zell and Genée turned out the sort of thing which Vienna might be supposed to enjoy, but they never did for Strauss, or even for the material which might be supposed to lie in their hand, what Meilhac and Halévy did for Offenbach. Vienna could well have afforded a counterpart to "La Vie Parisienne", and yet Strauss wasted his energies on inferior and ephemeral "books".

Nevertheless the serious study which men like Lange and Decsey have accorded the music of them, one and all, brings out much that is of great interest in the development of Strauss' genius and of Strauss as an aspirant to real operatic writing. It is a pity that out of so rich a treasury of music so comparatively little is ever heard to-day. The "Kommen und Geh'n", out of "Der Lustige Krieg", and the song Girardi made so famous could well deputise sometimes, surely, for those few overtures and waltzes of Strauss which are so well-known and given so often that it would almost seem as if he had never written anything else!

CHAPTER XVIII

JUBILEE, '84

IT is quite possible that the Blue Danube has ceased to to be Strauss' most popular waltz simply because it is so frequently given. But of the six or eight best known remaining waltzes which are being constantly put on the air in this country, it would be hard to say which is the most captivating. None of them ever stale!

If there is one gem of unsullied purity and freshness among all the rest, surely it is the "Frühlingstimme" (the Voices of Spring). This was a "concert-waltz". It was furnished with verses by Genée, and sung for the first time by the coloratura singer, Bianca Bianchi, on the occasion of a matinée at the Theater-an-der-Wien. The more engrossed Strauss became in his work for the stage, the more seldom he undertook this type of isolated composition, but the dances he wrote during the 'eighties show him at his very best. Among those were the "Nordseebilder" (Pictures of the North Sea), the "Myrtenblüten" (Myrtle-blossoms) and this lovely "Frühlingstimme".

These "Voices of Spring" depict the first carpeting of the ground under the bare trees of the forest, with every dainty blossom which first peeps through the sod. The gnarled convolutions of immense black roots are graced with all the woodland gems which blow in the gay breezes of spring, which spread sheets of colour in first floods of springtime sunshine. In this waltz we have the English flowers, if we like to think so, snowdrops and celandine and wood sorrel, anemones and primroses and violets, daffodils and cuckoo pint. . . . And amid them all white-clad maidens go, dancing with bare feet and hair unbound, care-free and virginal, to the trilling and fluting of the birds. The "Frühlingstimme" is a paradise of youth and innocence, an ecstasy of blue eyes waking to the morn.

The piece was far more immediately appreciated abroad, in Russia and Italy, than it was on production in Vienna. It departed too widely, perhaps, from the sparkle and vivacity of the style of music Strauss was writing for his operettas.

It required to be popularised before the Kaiserstadt quite understood it.

Together with their idolised Strauss, the Viennese possessed at this time a whole host of musical gods, before whom they were burning incense. There was, for instance, the wonderful Dalmatian, Franz von Suppé, who wrote the "Poet and Peasant".

But the art of the moment, influenced by Wagner and Brückner, was aiming chiefly at the vast and majestic in form. Success seemed to lie in the overpowering. The imposing operas of Goldmark attracted the newly-rich, who hastened from all quarters of the city to display themselves and their prosperity in the Opera House, while the smaller circle of the musical intelligentsia was swept off its feet by the brilliance of the Makart. There there was Millöcker, a delightful composer whose work in the spheres of light opera was fit to compete with that of the great Johann.

Dozens of men, gifted or necessitous, or both, were turning out operettas in Vienna, as elsewhere butchers turn out sausages; all were striving to make some spectacular hit like the "Fledermaus". Vienna had use for them all, and rejoiced in their fertility and their melodies, but for the most part their sucesses were fleeting.

It can be well understood what a nervous fever seized

these gentlemen whenever it chanced to get about that
somebody or other had written a first-class libretto! What
plans were laid, by hook or by crook, to get hold of it!
Everybody was convinced that the success of an operetta
depended upon an artistic unity as betwixt text and music.
However good the one might be, if the other failed it,
the work was doomed. No one had had more striking
experience of this than Strauss.

The Zell-Genée firm of librettists, the most important in
the city, (directed by Camillo Walzel), had recently produced two books and were anxious to place them most
advantageously. One was called "Der Bettelstudent"
(The Beggar Student), and the other "Eine Nacht in
Venedig" (A Night in Venice). A competitor of Strauss,
Karl Millöcker, managed to get hold of both scripts, and
immediately recognised the attractive possibilities and the
superiority of the first named. Planking his hand down upon
the "Bettelstudent", he declared he could do without
the other if he couldn't have this. Because, of course,
Johann Strauss considered he should be accorded the right
of first choice.

What in the world would happen now, wondered the
partners, if the greater of the two great men were also to
decide for the "Bettelstudent"! For, of course, Strauss
must be given his choice.

And this is exactly what happened.

Strauss also decided to score the "Bettelstudent", without having any idea that he had been so far slighted as to
have had the books submitted to him only in the second
place.

The librettists saved themselves from an impossible
situation by a ruse worthy of one of their own operettas.
They were obliged to own up that Millöcker had already
seen the two pieces and was vastly in hopes that Strauss

would *not* decide for the "Night in Venice". This was quite enough to give Johann pause as to his preference for the other book. He felt Millöcker's choice might well be more fortunate than any decision of his own. Whereupon he had little scruple about reversing it. He informed the partners that he preferred the "Night in Venice" on the whole, and they might accordingly submit the "Bettel-student" to any other client of theirs they liked.

Zell and Genée were immensely relieved, and it is to be presumed they kept their little secret to themselves as well as Johann kept his. None of them, apparently, had the faintest scruple about the matter.

That it really might have been as easy as this to throw dust into Strauss' eyes, and that he so radically distrusted his own judgment as to be willing to do another man out of the better piece in this way, goes to show how fierce was the artistic competition in Vienna at this time.

Strauss had better have stuck to his own first impressions of the two librettos. In the event it turned out that the "Bettelstudent" was the better piece, by far. And Millöcker scored an immense hit with it. The "Night in Venice" only turned out a disappointment. Again, the text let the music down.

Strauss scored it, bringing all his impressions of Italy to bear upon his work, and all the old Austrian conception of the lost province of Venezia as a veritable paradise, but the audience, who looked for a good story as well as for a Strauss setting, detected a thousand sillinesses and weaknesses in Zell and Genée's latest fabrication, and did not hesitate to say so. It was produced in Berlin (3rd October, 1883) but the supposition that this was so because Strauss would have no more to do with the Theater-an-der-Wien can hardly be maintained, since it appeared on the old boards in Vienna only a week after.

Like so many of Strauss' librettos, it had to be tinkered about a good deal later on, but even then it had no particular success. One or two numbers had to be cut out, the words were so excessively silly. Finally, however, the text underwent a thorough overhauling for the sake of saving the music; the famous waltz "Künstlerleben" (Artist's Life) was substituted for a comic song, and the "Night in Venice" survived the partial failure of its Berlin début. It became one of the stock pieces in the repertory of the Viennese theatre.

.   .   .   .   .

The poetic justice of early disillusionment befell Angelika Strauss. The man for whom she left her husband seems to have had no intention of marrying her. She was soon abandoned. But now it was too late to dream of reconciliation. Johann, unable to tolerate a bachelor existence, and inflammable of heart as ever, had already fallen in love again—quite sincerely, and with the most honest of intentions. As it turned out, his last matrimonial venture was quite the most suitable, and perhaps the happiest of the three.

Years ago in the Hirschenhaus two families of the name of Strauss, but unrelated, had been friends and neighbours. A Herr Albert Strauss, a banker, had often given Johann the elder the benefit of his advice in business and other matters. A son of his, Anton, had married a charming Viennese girl called Adèle Deutsch, but had died within three years leaving her with a little daughter, Alice. Adèle was broken-hearted. She withdrew into retirement and it was years before she got over her loss.

In 1883 she was still comparatively young, and good-looking. A chance encounter with the lion of Vienna, that very Johann Strauss she had known as a child, with whose rather foolish name gossip had had so much to do of late, led suddenly to the remaking of an old acquaintance.

Johann had been driving over the Ferdinandsbrücke one day when he caught sight of a vaguely familiar figure in black. He lifted his hat to the lady, who gave him a friendly smile of recognition in return. It was Adèle of course, old Herr Albert's widowed daughter-in-law.

Somehow her face came between the composer and his work. The score of the "Nacht in Venedig" lay upon Strauss' desk, but the thought of Adèle distracted his attention. Rather unaccountably, it must have seemed, Johann began to find frequent occasion to visit his sisters in the Hirschenhaus, and to frequent the apartment of their neighbour. When the latter's daughter-in-law also began to be a little more attentive to him than usual, and when her visits were observed to coincide somewhat markedly with those of the prodigal celebrity, Herr Albert must have been less astute than people supposed him, not to have seen what was afoot.

When the pair came out into the open and acknowledged an ardent attraction to each other, the suggestion of a marriage between them aroused strong domestic opposition, probably on both sides. Strauss was nominally a Catholic but Frau Adèle was a Jewess. The newly-arisen situation was fraught with difficulties of all kinds. The Lily problem had to be tackled and settled, and this involved such legal and religious complications that Strauss, willing to take any extravagant steps to achieve his purpose, even went to the length of changing his nationality and his religious profession. He left Vienna for a time and went to live at Coburg, at that time the capital of the Dukedom (Herzogtums) of Sachsen-Coburg-Gotha, and became a Protestant. The Emperor Franz Josef found it particularly hard to forgive him on both counts.

Lily Strauss did her utmost to distress and embarrass everybody. She took to wandering about in the neighbourhood of the house at Schönau, posing as an injured and rejected wife, until legal interference brought her back to things as they really were.

Johann contrived to contract this third alliance somehow. The wedding took place on German soil, and in due course Strauss was back in his palace in the Igelgasse working on his latest operetta.

Frau Adèle restored his home to the old semblance of its happiest self in the Jetty period. She was an excellent manager and housekeeper, an accomplished woman of society, and was fitted in every way to surround her husband with such comfort, and to accord him such complete artistic sympathy and understanding, that he forthwith embarked on a brilliant period of rejuvenation and musical success.

Her daughter, Alice, brought a note into his life and home which it had hitherto lacked. Strauss was much attached to her, and wrote one of his most charming compositions for the festivities attendant on her marriage later.

It was now that he did away with the flowing side whiskers which had carried him so successfully through the "Dundreary" period of masculine foppishness. He shaved himself clean, save for a bushy moustache, turned up, but not waxed, at the ends. His hair was still luxuriant and leonine, even if art had to be called in to maintain its glossy blackness. He was fifty-nine, and at the height of his mature powers.

During the last two decades of his life Strauss was almost overwhelmed by the number and magnificence of a whole series of Jubilees which now began to be accorded him. Johann was at heart a modest man, and this sort of thing was by no means agreeable to him. Besides, it smacked

a little bit too much of the flight of time! He would have
avoided the Jubilees, one and all, if possible. But it was not
possible. Vienna, Austria, Berlin, Germany—all Europe
and America vied with each other in doing honour to the
Waltz King. In October, 1884, Vienna organised a great
fête to celebrate the fortieth anniversary of his début at
Dommayer's Café.

In the course of his career Johann had encountered much
encouragement, and much spectacular success, but it must
by no means be supposed that he had not also been made
the object of much personal and professional criticism. His
work had, indeed, been as virulently and as adversely, and
as persistently criticised (or what is worse at times, faintly
praised), as that of any man who has had original things
to say in music, and who has chosen an original way of
saying them. Johann's genius was developing all through
his life. Every phase of it had been attacked by the con-
servative, the envious, or the merely superficial among the
musical critics of his time. Their admonitions and their
reproofs read strangely to-day. But Strauss survived his
mentors not merely artistically, but physically. He lived
to see his own triumph and his own fame.

On this particular day he drove through cheering flag-
bedecked Vienna, under triumphal arches and along the
gaily decorated boulevards, to receive addresses of official
congratulation here, there and everywhere, but far more
to be the object of the universal acclaim of a whole population. He had become, for the Kaiserstadt, the very embodiment of all that was brightest and gayest and happiest
in the very air and spirit of Vienna.

In the Igelgasse, "Croquet", Strauss' favourite dog, had
to be safely shut up somewhere until further orders, for the
doors of the Meister's house had to be flung wide open for
the reception of an endless series of deputations. All the

organisations of Vienna, civic, musical, theatrical, professional, came to congratulate him, and present addresses.
The Burgomaster Uhl came (Johann was presented with the
Freedom of the City of Vienna), the Society of the Friends
of Music, the Viennese Men's Choral Society, and a dozen
others. The Master was snowed under with letters, greetings
and telegrams from all quarters of the globe. Gifts came
from many of his more intimate personal friends, from
Bismarck, Billroth, Brahms, Millöcker, Suppé and Verdi.
In the evening he had to be smuggled somehow into the
Theater-an-der-Wien, where he was to direct a programme
of music from his own works, from an orchestra positively
buried in flowers. When he appeared, the enthusiasm was
indescribable. It seemed as if he would never be allowed
to raise his baton to begin. The people utterly exhausted
themselves in cheering and applauding. They clapped till
their hands were sore, roared till they were hoarse, pelted
flowers until there were no more to pelt, and stamped on
the floor till it rocked.

His friends were there in full force, together with Prince
Orlofski, the Warder Frosch, Adèle, Rosalind, all the ball
guests from the famous second Act of "Fledermaus",
together with Arthur Bryk and Marie, out of the "Carnival
in Rome", "Cagliostro", "Prince Methuselah" and more
and ever more characters out of his own well-beloved
operettas.

Strauss directed the music—selections from all these
works, together with "The Blue Danube" and all those
other lovely numbers of his whose names had long since
passed into household words throughout Europe and
America.

At last, almost exhausted with the fatigue of taking his
incessant and merciless curtains, he stood up to speak,
struggling to command a voice which trembled with tears.

"I am too deeply touched," he said, "to be able to put feelings which are indescribable into words. For now I can only sum them up by this—I thank you all, my beloved fellow citizens of Vienna, from the very depths of my overfull heart!"

Whereupon the storm broke loose again. After this came a banquet in the famous Hotel Lamm, in the Leopoldstadt, when fish from the beautiful Blue Danube was served, the guests disappeared in showers of Italian confetti. Strauss was made the recipient of more medals and diplomas than he could count, so that it was an overburdened man indeed, one overburdened with the congratulations and recognition of his fellow men, who fell back in the early hours of the morning upon his bed, when the Jubilee was mercifully over!

In September, 1885, the Friedrich Wilhelm Theater, in Berlin, invited him to conduct a three days' "Strauss Fête"; and then again, later, it organised a whole month of Strauss music. In this case Strauss was unable to be present, as he was engaged upon a new work at home, and could allow nothing to divert him from it.

To anticipate a little—in 1894 another great Jubilee was accorded him in recognition of his fifty years of music. It was the most tremendous of all. Cascades of flowers poured into the Igelgasse, letters, presents, many of them with no other inscription than "To the Waltz King".

Again, all the artists of the day hastened to send congratulations. The students of the Conservatorium of Music serenaded him, and endless deputations beset his house and his reception rooms as before. A ballet of Strauss music was given in the Court Opera House. American musicians sent him a silver wreath of myrtle leaves fifty in number, with the name of one of his works inscribed upon each. A band of Hawaiian musicians in Honolulu sent him a group photograph of themselves. Strauss was more deeply and more widely beloved than any other Austrian artist had ever been before him. A comic weekly, the *Figaro*, published a drawing of him, showing him quite exhausted by all these festivities given in his honour, wrapped in a dressing gown and assuring himself "If all this doesn't turn my hair grey, nothing will!" But the glorious black lion locks of Johann Strauss had become symbolic. Vienna knew, quite well, they would never turn grey. And they never did.

Over and over again he had to support these monster Jubilees.

CHAPTER XIX

ZIGEUNERBARON, '85

WITH the "Gypsy Baron" (24th October, 1885) Johann Strauss obtained as great a success as with the "Bat" eleven years previously.

And the "Gypsy Baron" serves as well as anything Strauss ever wrote to illustrate the claim that has been made for him as the musical peacemaker of his time. In this work he did something for the two halves of Franz Josef's awkward empire, for Austria and for Hungary, which neither the Emperor nor his ministers had been able to accomplish.

In the long course of one of the saddest and most dramatic reigns history has ever seen, Franz Josef tried one experiment after another to hold the Dual Monarchy together. None but a somewhat close student of the conflicting affairs of Central Europe all through the nineteenth century, is in any position to qualify the commonly accepted conception of every Habsburg sovereign as an autocrat and reactionary. While Franz Josef was a typical Habsburg, it cannot, however, be denied that he did make many attempts to understand the people over whom he ruled, and that time and again he listened to progressive-minded statesmen who would make some tentative gestures in a liberal way.

Ever since the settlement of Europe after Elba, Austria had been busy extending her Empire over nations not belonging to the Teutonic stock. She had receded from Germany, and held herself aloof, under Prince Metternich, from the repeated efforts made elsewhere after this constitutional idea. As we have seen in an earlier chapter, the news of the revolution in France excited rebellions in many other countries. Kossuth, in Hungary (which still enjoyed a constitutional Government), pronounced a violent speech against the Austrian Government which led to the Revolution in Vienna in 1848. After that, Austria undertook a campaign against Hungary which might not have succeeded in reducing the country, had she not called in the assistance of Russia.

The Emperor it was, however, who made an attempt next year to re-organise his dominions. He published a Constitution. Nothing, of course, remotely like liberty was established anywhere, and it still remained true for the whole of Austria, that the best citizen was he who discreetly took no interest in politics. The Empress Elizabeth was much drawn to the Hungarian people, and was much beloved by them. When, in 1866, the Prussians were threatening Vienna, Elizabeth and the young Crown Prince Rudolf withdrew for safety across the Hungarian frontier. They were warmly received by Franz Deak and other Hungarian notabilities, and it was doubtless largely due to circumstances of this sort that the two countries were eventually reconciled, and Hungary regained her previous footing. Franz Josef and the Empress were crowned King and Queen of Hungary at Pressburg—now Budapest—on the 8th of June, 1867. But, for all this, Austria and Hungary remained uneasy and ill-yoked neighbours. The two halves of the monarchy were for ever at variance, and stubbornly unable to arrive at workable compromises. To what did these everlasting journeys of ministers to and fro lead? What was the use of these deputations, and delegations and political comedies of every sort?

MONUMENT TO STRAUSS, VIENNA.

It needed something very different to bring Austrian and Hungarian together.

It needed Strauss!

An operetta of the Viennese master gave the two quarrelsome neighbours something in common, in the enjoyment of which they could lay aside their strife. He wrote the music for a comedy half-Hungarian, half-Viennese, which created a friendly atmosphere, a pleasant undertone, which did not remain without effect even in the council chamber.

Franz von Jauner, now the Director of the Theater-an-der-Wien, went to immense expense and put himself to great pains to dress and stage "The Gypsy Baron" in the true Hungarian style. He made a journey to Raab to study a real gypsy encampment on the spot, and brought back with him to Vienna the original blind horse and its waggon which figure in the play, and the original costumes of the chorus. He was aiming at an absolutely realistic setting. So much so, that Strauss himself was led to hope for the success of the work, if only on account of the scenario!

The story of how he came by this libretto is easier to relate than that of the extraordinary amalgam itself. The "Zigeunerbaron" may have appealed vividly enough to the audiences for whom it was written, especially as it offered parts full of fun and possibility for the principal singers, and for Girardi in particular. But unlike "Fledermaus", independent of locality or period, the "Zigeunerbaron" was a Hungarian piece winding up in the baroque Vienna of the Maria Theresa period, and so the humour of it, and the point, and the topicality are lost for us in this country to-day. The types in it—richly significant and amusing for Budapest and Vienna in 1885—are wholly strange and alien to us. They comprised gypsies, soldiers, stiff Austrian officials, melancholy or intoxicated Magyars, cheerful illiterates, pig-breeding rascals, queer damsels, nomads who became princes, and all the rest of the stock in trade of the lighter opera of the time.

A number of propitious circumstances brought this "book" into existence. In 1883 Strauss went to Budapest to conduct a performance of his "Merry War". There he visited the great Hungarian novelist, Maurus Jokai, with a view to obtaining a work from him which could be scored for the theatre. Some time after his return to Vienna, Jokai sent him a libretto based upon his novel *Saffi*. Strauss thought it lacking in action, and was at a loss to see how it could be suitably adapted for his purpose. Nevertheless the very man for this work was at hand. A Hungarian journalist, Ignaz Schnitzer, who lived in Vienna, had once before approached Strauss about an operetta he had written in collaboration with another man. Nothing came of the matter at the time. But, with Johann puzzling his head over Hungarian stuff, it was quite possible that Albert Strauss at the Hirschenhaus remembered Schnitzer, and reintroduced him. The journalist was an admirable adapter and translator, and an ardent Hungarian. Moreover he was highly musical, had an eye for good situations, could readily set verses to a given melody, and was qualified to be of much assistance to the composer.

Strauss was willing to see what Schnitzer could do with Jokai's *Saffi*, and Schnitzer made of it the outstanding success of his career. The novelist was extremely loath to allow his name to appear in connection with the end product of Schnitzer's literary activities, the "Zigeunerbaron", so completely had the adapter knocked the original to pieces. But Strauss made a great point of it, and Jokai gave way.

The story appealed tremendously to Schnitzer. It opened at the time when the Turks were withdrawing from the fast disappearing world that had been old Hungary. One of their last Pashas had fled, leaving his daughter and an immense treasure behind him. There was scope in all this for any amount of romance and phantasy, for tears and love and laughter.

The work on this operetta was a novel and very pleasurable experience for Strauss. For the first time perhaps, he found himself in accord with his literary colleague, and delivered over to the scoring of a work far superior in quality to the great bulk of all which had hitherto been offered him.

This is by no means to say that Strauss and Schnitzer were always agreed upon things. They had many a tussle, and sometimes the issue remained in abeyance for days. The Hungarian was quite artist enough to insist, in places, that Strauss should follow his advice.

Johann departed, over the "Zigeunerbaron", from his accustomed impetuosity of inspirational composition. He forced himself to unusual care and deliberation, took plenty of time about it, refused to let himself be side-tracked in any way, or hurried. Jokai was most anxious to have the operetta ready for production at some millennial festivities in Pesth, but Strauss allowed himself nearly two years (from the beginning of 1883 to the end of 1884), in which to complete the score. None of the music in the "Zigeunerbaron" should lay itself open to criticism on the ground of hastiness of conception, or of insufficient development. This was to approximate very nearly to the mature musical dignity of acknowledged opera.

Strauss composed the third act in Ostend.

The music for this work was written without being tied, literally, to the text. Much of it was composed in general harmony with the mise-en-scène, before the appropriate words, songs, duets, etc., had been allocated at all. Schnitzer followed Strauss, rather than expecting the composer to

follow the librettist. In this way Strauss was better able
to balance his effects, and judge of the requisite length of
his various motives. The opera was musically articulated
as it were, before it became vocal. Strauss was not particularly fond of what the German calls the "Possenhaft"
in his operetta, the tipsy clownishness which made of
Frosch in "Die Fledermaus" one of his outstanding
achievements. In "Der Zigeunerbaron" occurred another
such figure, a hog breeder, but here again, Girardi's
consummate conception of the part, helped to lift him
and it to the regions of fine art. At a somewhat earlier
period theatrical experience went to show that success
depended largely on the composer writing expressly for
this, that or the other singer, and not merely by way of
scoring a work in general. Strauss bore this fact in mind
when setting Jokai's libretto, and the actress, Fraülein
Collin, as Saffi, Streitmann as Barinkay, and above all
Girardi as the hog breeder, reaped the benefit of his ripe
artistry.

As usual, Strauss grew terribly nervy and apprehensive
as the rehearsals drew towards the end. More and more
was he convinced that the "Zigeunerbaron" would prove a
failure.

He went home the night before its production to night-
mares from which he awoke bathed in the sweat of anguish.
Adèle, who never forgot all she went through this awful
evening, kept him just the sort of sympathetic but calming
company, which was the boon he craved most of life. . . .

And then came the 24th of October, the eve of his sixtieth
birthday, and the First Night of this enigmatic "Zigeunerbaron."

All the prognostications of the optimists paled before
the accomplished fact. Never had the Theater-an-der-Wien
risen so enthusiastically to any piece before. The operetta

was given three times if it was given once, the encores
were so incessant and so vociferous. "Zigeunerbaron" was
a first-class artistic triumph, an undoubted theatrical hit,
and a splendid commercial coup.

Strauss, Schnitzer, Jauner and Co. had nothing more to
do but to congratulate themselves, and bask in the sun of
unqualified success.

CHAPTER XX

EVER since Strauss began writing operetta no more than two years had elapsed, at most, without a new production. "Cagliostro" followed "Fledermaus", and the "Merry War" followed the "Queen's Handkerchief", at intervals of a year.

So now again "The Gypsy Baron", written and produced in 1885, was followed in December, 1887, by "Simplizius."

Johann was always interested in the work of other men in his own field, and read the newspaper notices and criticisms of their productions with eagerness. But he seldom went to see them. He was very anxious for the reputation of his own originality. It is no contradiction to the claim made for him by everyone best in a position to know—that he was a man singularly free from professional envy and jealousy—to say that it upset him dreadfully to miss a good libretto. Plenty of theatrical successes were scored by other composers in Vienna during Strauss' time, and these sometimes at the very moment when a piece of his own perhaps was enjoying but a succès d'éstime.

In the year of the "Zigeunerbaron" Nessler's "Trompeter von Säkkingen" made a tremendous hit. As a result of this, Strauss was convinced that his next work must be a thoroughly German subject. A whole host of advisers and counsellors endeavoured to persuade him to the contrary—that just because the "Säkkingen" *was* so good he must in no way compete with it, but go as far afield as possible for his next theme, get a story from the Arctic or from Brazil, or anywhere so long as it was not German!

Strauss, however, was not to be moved from his own idea. He was in correspondence with Maurus Jokai about a new libretto, and in collaboration with Schnitzer over an opera of which the first act had already been written, when he heard of something very novel by a man called Victor Léon, "Der Doppelgänger" (The Double) which had just been produced with much success in Munich.

Victor Léon was a young writer who aimed at revolutionising the theatre. He believed in "serious operetta", in which human passions rather than invented situations should constitute the chief interest of a play. This was just before German naturalism came into vogue. Strauss felt that Léon's first attempt along new and revolutionary lines should be followed up by a second. He despatched a friend to the young man to open up negotiations. The writer was all but overwhelmed by the compliment, the favour, the prospect! The great composer had seen his "Doppelgänger" and wanted to know if he had written anything else of a similar character? If so would he dine at the Igelgasse one evening in the near future, and discuss ideas?

Léon arrived, nervous and eager, armed with half-a-dozen works. Strauss turned them over appraisingly, pausing here and there for consideration, and then enquired what his guest might be working upon at the moment. Whereupon the other launched into an enthusiastic and dramatic account of a popular story he had taken from the period of the Thirty Years War and adapted for the stage under the title "Simplizius", (The Country Bumpkin). Strauss was delighted with it. But unfortunately the piece was already placed. It was the same story as the "Bettelstudent" all over again.

Zamara had the first claim on this book.

Possibly Strauss was only doing what every other composer in Vienna would also do, and condone, in snatching a likely libretto from another. In this case a new agreement had to be arranged at once in favour of Strauss, although the date had actually been fixed for the production of the work by Zamara, in Munich, and the singer chosen for the title rôle!

The main idea of this piece was that of a countrified fellow transformed by love into a hero.

Strauss hoped great things of his new undertaking, but as the work proceeded, certain doubts about it crept into his mind. The problem was a difficult one, how to introduce a serious note into the gay and melodious medley always demanded by a Viennese audience. Strauss devoted himself to the task so keenly that he refused to go to Berlin where a great 'Strauss Cycle' was being given in the Friedrich-Wilhelmstadt Theatre. He handed over the music at last, without describing the work as opera or operetta to the Theater-an-der-Wien, and everybody's anticipations rose to fever point.

Immense hopes were set upon this innovation. The publisher offered Léon 20,000 gulden for his share, but the writer declined this and other offers, relying wholly on the genius of Strauss. The experts prophesied great things for "Simplizius", just as they had anticipated failure for the "Zigeunerbaron". No one can ever tell how things theatrical will turn out.

The work was produced on the 17th of December, 1887. The audience saw every beauty in it except gaiety, for even that of the music seemed forced.

For Strauss had detected a new problem in the thing he had attempted to do, the problem of the serious musical play. Years had elapsed since he turned his attention to the theatre, and immense developments had been taking place meanwhile. As composer his inspiration was full and free as ever, but he had attained to no new conception of form. Things operatic had developed without carrying him along in their course, and his voluntary isolation began to tell.

Strauss ran aground, as others ran aground, on a problem which was one of the time and the moment. "Simplizius" fell between two stools in style. Again it was a far cry from the irresistible merriment and bubbling fun of "Fledermaus", to the almost artificial gaiety and naïveté of "Simplizius".

Strauss had been writing music for over forty years. When at work upon a score he was seldom satisfied with an output of less than twenty or thirty sheets a day. He had surmounted many semi-disappointments with equanimity, and almost unimpaired ardour. No artist ever wept less over spilt milk. As soon as one piece was written and forgotten, he flung himself with pristine optimism into the next. "Simplizius" counted among his semi-failures in spite of its many excellencies, and although Strauss himself cared a great deal for the work he had put into it, not only because of its artistry, but for a far more immediate reason. On the first night of its production a fire broke out in the theatre which would soon have led to panic, but for the presence of mind of none other than the man who was sometimes looked upon as a neurasthenic himself at the conductor's podium. Like many highly nervous people, Strauss could command himself at a crisis. Amid shouts and cries people were already stampeding to the exits: everybody was terrified of a catastrophe like that of the Ring Theatre, not so very long ago. But Strauss spiritedly struck up an encore to one of the waltz songs which had just brought down the house, and the applause which again broke through the tumult helped him still further to pacify the audience. Things quieted down, and the evening was saved.

"Simplizius" was beautiful, but enigmatic. The gems in it went into the Strauss treasury, and the text was radically altered and edited later, but it cannot be said that the work ever attained much popularity.

In 1889 Strauss "acquitted himself of a debt which he had acknowledged warmly all his life". He brought out a comprehensive collection of his father's works. It was published by the firm of Breitkopf and Härtel, and contained a delightful preface from his own pen which gave many particulars of his father's and Lanner's interesting methods of composition.

In the same year he went to Berlin and conducted five great concerts there, although he had long relinquished this type of work in Vienna, having left it entirely in the hands of his brother Edouard.

Four years elapsed between "Simplizius" and the next work Strauss wrote for the musical stage. At no previous time had so long an interval interrupted the series of his operettas. But it is to be remembered that so terrible a tragedy overtook Vienna and all Austria in the January of 1889, that even Strauss' powers would have failed to relieve the general gloom. The Crown Prince Rudolf was found dead under mysterious and tragic circumstances in his shooting box at Mayerling. He had been greatly beloved by the Austrian people, who saw in him a cultured man of modern ideas, who would do much for the country once he came to the throne. He would probably have proved to the world that a Habsburg monarch was capable of conceiving the democratic ideal, and of carrying it out in his Government. His death, and the horror and scandal of it, convulsed Europe. It threw a shadow over the sufficiently sombre life of the Empress Elizabeth from which she never emerged again.

·   ·   ·   ·   ·

Strauss was getting very weary of the type of production which contained so little artistry, that it had to be knocked about by all sorts of people, besides the librettist and composer, before it could be given. He was getting very weary, too, of always having to constrain his own art within the limits dictated by popular appraisal and monetary success. It had been conditioned and belittled too long by the medium he had chosen. Strauss wanted to write something more musically important, something in the direction of serious opera, something which gave scope to the best of which he was capable.

He played for some time with the idea of a Shakespearean theme based on Viola in "As You Like It", but this was dispelled by his meeting with a young Hungarian writer, Ludwig Doczi, who had recently scored a great success at the Burg Theatre with a piece called "The Kiss". Strauss was now fired with the ardent hope that this Ludwig Doczi might furnish him with a suitable libretto. There is something pathetic in the way Strauss always seems to have been dazzled by the idea that a success would repeat itself. He dropped Viola for a feeble story about another kiss, just because of a success of that name at the Burg Theatre! There is something intriguing, too, about the speculation as to what would have resulted had Strauss ever found exactly the right librettist!

Only twice, perhaps, in the whole series of his operettas, was he really happy in his texts.

The story of "Ritter Pasman" forms no exception to the general rule.

People were amazed that the Master (as he much disliked to be called), ever imagined it could sustain the wealth of melody with which he embellished it. They could not understand his accepting such a text at all. It was not wanting in beauty, nor perhaps in good scenes,

but it lacked lightness and humour, and was ill-suited to
Strauss.

An Hungarian King whilst hunting in the domains of
one of his vassals, the Ritter Pasman, is entertained at
the castle and falls in love with his beautiful wife, Eva.
Taking advantage of a temporary absence of the Knight,
the impetuous King seizes the lady and impresses an ardent
kiss upon her lips. One of the knight's squires who espied
the incident, reveals it to Pasman on his return. Pasman
is enraged, he curses his wife, and sets off in hot pursuit
of the royal delinquent.

The third act opens with the Knight appearing before
the King to avenge his honour. This King, however, is
none other in reality than the Court Jester, who had
hurriedly changed clothes with his lord. He hears the
knight's charge, and answers it by decreeing that Pasman
shall impress a kiss, in his turn, upon the brow of the
Queen. Pasman is about to do so when the rightful King
bursts in, and immediately orders him to be flung into
the dungeon. But the Queen pacifies her husband, and
graciously sets her own lips to the forehead of the knight
who had but sought to uphold the stainlessness of his
name!

All this struck the Strausses and their circle of intimates—
to whom Frau Adèle read it—as very graceful and poetic.
They were charmed with it, and praised its many captivating
passages. The Master really thought he had found exactly
the "book" he wanted this time! He shut himself up in his
study, refused all invitations and visitors, and devoted
himself to the task of scoring it. He was aiming now at
his ultimate artistic goal. And as far as the music went,
indeed, he reached it.

The opera "Ritter Pasman" was the work of a composer
aged sixty-six, and yet it was to a great extent a new

departure. His gifts were of a special and peculiar order, and in this work he was turning them to new and serious account. A critic wrote at the time, "What is so particularly admirable about "Ritter Pasman" is its sustained earnestness, and the energy with which its character is maintained throughout. It is more than a piece of artistry, it is a self-revelation on the part of the composer . . . which demands our greatest respect even if in parts we do not find it wholly pleasing." If the success of "Pasman" had been great enough to encourage Strauss to continue writing opera, he might indeed have developed the grander style so far as finally to surmount the drawback which his text always offered to his music. "Opera, like a symphony, is an architectural problem," and the writer must recognise this equally with the composer. The ballet scene in "Pasman" was the only one which offered full facility to Strauss. The music here reached its highest pitch of beauty and perfection, so that the rest of the opera was merely written around it. Relieved of the "text", this part of the score was far too valuable, as music, to be consigned to those archives of musical history "in which the dead survive but have no resurrection". Gustav Mahler sought Strauss' permission later on to write something wholly fresh for it, but the attempt was found impracticable. Doczi himself undertook a revision of "Simplizius", but in vain, like all attempts at resuscitation.

"Ritter Pasman" was awaited with much eagerness by the public, and its production at the Hofoperntheater on the 1st of January, 1892, created a sensation. Every resource of theatrical art and management had been used in its mounting, and the cast was practically an all-star one. It met with a spasmodically enthusiastic reception, and had but a qualified success. "What we miss in this higher sphere," wrote Hanslick, "is by no means the accomplished man of taste and first-class musician—but simply, our old beloved Johann Strauss!"

"Ritter Pasman" was withdrawn after nine performances at the Opera House, and it never achieved a greater success elsewhere.

Strauss, with an equanimity which must certainly be reckoned among his most admirable characteristics, made no great matter of this comparative failure. He had, for once, written the music he most desired and most strove to write, and felt a high degree of satisfaction in having at least dared to do the best that was in him. Strauss cut his artistic losses gracefully, and proceeded without plaint or apparent regret to write ever more and more music.

"Let bygones be bygones," he remarked to a friend. "I know well enough how to survive it! One thing I am glad of, and that is that no one accused me of 'triviality' in 'Pasman'! It can't be supposed to lie at my door that the public cared so little for an old Hungarian story and that the 'text' was thin. In any case I set more store by the smallest success of an opera of mine than by anything else."

Frau Adèle shielded him, as far as a solicitous wife might, from too much disturbing criticism. She took him away from Vienna for a while, and they spent the following summer in his villa at Ischl, where they entertained a succession of their more intimate friends, and no doubt had an extremely delightful time.

CHAPTER XXI

AFTER "Pasman" the general consensus of opinion drove Strauss back to operetta. Even had he wished to do so, his friends, his public, and his critics would never have allowed the Waltz King to abandon his last. It is a curious phenomenon in the artistic life, and one often to be observed, how a man who has made an immense success in one particular direction, comes to detest it in exact proportion to his admirers' demand that he should pursue this path and this alone. Gilbert and Sullivan are classic examples in Strauss' own field. "Sherlock Holmes" is another in the literary life. Johann aspired to serious opera, and his whole world clamoured to recall him not only to operetta but to the waltz.

It was easy enough for him to respond. The air of Vienna was ever all around him, and his inspiration knew no flagging. Had he not written "Pasman" he would have fallen short of the greatest and finest he could do. This fact adds immense interest to the occasional selections from Strauss' one opera with which the Radio may sometimes favour us. It is to be wished, however, that this music were better known by the English listening public, and associated with his name as familiarly as the "Voices of Spring" or "The Tales of the Vienna Woods". "Pasman" would have been the composer's own choice of a monument to his memory.

A year later "Fürsten Ninetta" (Princess Ninetta) was produced in the Theater-an-der-Wien. This was quite a

slight thing, but it had a good seasonal success, and delighted
the Emperor, who personally congratulated the composer
afterwards. Strauss had now entered into a contract with
a new firm of librettists. These gentlemen submitted "texts"
to him, whose mediocrity could only be accounted for on
the ground of their extreme anxiety in the face of too much
competition.

Next came "Jabuka" (October, 1894), which served to
usher in the immense festivities of the beloved composer's
fifty year Jubilee.

With perfectly astonishing fertility, and the ready
fervour of youth Strauss produced "Waldmeister" the
following December.

It would serve little purpose to outline the slight stories
of these operettas. Not one of them is worth it. Strauss'
music is always Strauss' music, but there was nothing
immortal about these scores.

Unfortunately a grave quarrel with Girardi had preceded
the first night of "Waldmeister", so that the singer refused
to appear. He had long since become entitled to permit
himself the outrageous tantrums of a first-class operatic
star, and he seems to have exercised the right on this
occasion. People had upset him.

Strauss managed to bring him to reason, and the evening
passed off successfully, bringing nothing but fresh laurels
to all the principals concerned. Like the preceding operetta,
and like the next, "Waldmeister" was a seasonal success.

In March, a couple of years later, Strauss produced his
sixteenth operetta, "Die Göttin der Vernunft" (The Goddess
of Reason). Two men, Willner and Buchbinder, had collaborated to produce a story of the time of the French Revolution. The composer, however, cared so little for it, and
thought so little of it, that he never even attended its first
night. It was very well put on and heartily pleased the

audience, but was nevertheless a failure. It never repeated the success of its début.

All the later operettas of Strauss were merely pieces which ran for a while during the winter, and disappeared with the spring. Their historical and artistic interest lies chiefly in the fact that they portrayed a society which was even then passing away. They belonged to the last decade of the last century, and to the last stage of the civic metamorphosis of pre-war Vienna. The Linienwälle, the city's last confines dating from the era of the Turkish menace, were now thrown down, and ten of the outer districts were incorporated with the city proper. Together with the original ten districts they now formed New Vienna, or Great Vienna, as the Strauss waltz had it, which he wrote for a ball to be given in the Concordia during this time. A new society surged into the city through these extensive breaches. The destruction of her old confines was symbolic of the destruction of much of her old nineteenth century tradition. "The people began to become class-conscious, and the old framework of society commenced to feel the strain. The feudal aristocracy at the top broke away from the Jewish financial circles, and social democracy came into being as the enemy of both. A new society, armed with new weapons, struck down the old acceptances and the old distinctions. The Popular Concert vied now with the exclusive Philharmonic Orchestra of former days, and the People's Opera threw down the gauntlet to the privileged Court Opera."[1] As time went on, the new form of operetta came to be linked with Strauss' tradition only by the thinnest of ties.

Johann Strauss had begun as a writer of dances, chiefly waltzes, and as the conductor of an orchestra always at the nod and beck of the entertainment caterers. He went from

[1] Redlich.

success to success, ever climbing higher and higher in a joyous but very arduous profession. He became an outstanding figure in light-hearted Vienna, and presently a "Master" of European renown, and of transatlantic idolatry. In his progress he was led to abandon first, dance writing pure and simple, and second, orchestra conducting, in favour of devoting the bulk of his time and energies to composing for the stage. After "Ritter Pasman", which was too highbrow for its public, the cry arose for Strauss to go back to his waltzes. After "Die Göttin der Vernunft", all Vienna begged him to turn his attention to the ballet.

Nothing loath, Strauss fell to work with a will, and began to do something new of this sort on a big scale for Herr Hassreiter, the popular ballet director to the Court Opera. It was to be called "Aschenbrödel" (Cinderella).

It so happened, however, that on Monday in Whitsunweek, May 22nd, 1899, as he was conducting the overture to "Fledermaus" at a matinée, he took a chill. He was often obliged to give up the baton after the opening of a piece, and to relinquish the conductor's desk, owing to the profuse sweat which attended the excitement of the initial movements. At the last bar he instantly disappeared to avoid the storm of applause. For the moment that slender, polished figure made its appearance, with its spirited head and untamed black hair, the moment those dark gypsy-like eyes flashed fire over the orchestra, and the thin, nervous hand raised the baton, the audience rose at it with unappeasable enthusiasm. Everyone present was resolved to see Strauss, and applaud him, cost what it might!

When he drove home to the Igelgasse on this particular day his linen was found to be wet through. He changed, had a good rub-down, and then engaged in a game of Tarock with a couple of friends, not in the garden but in a room giving on to it.

He felt no ill-effects from the profuse sweat he had undergone at the theatre, and betook himself as usual to his
study in the evening, in order to go on with Cinderella.
The work was making good progress, and he planned to
take it to Ischl very shortly and finish it at his villa
there.

A few days later he attended a fête in the neighbourhood
of Vienna, and with his usual geniality autographed a number
of fans in aid of its object. Shortly after this he was taken
with a rigor, followed by some degree of fever. He was
obliged to go to bed.

The master of the ballet called to see him on business
about "Aschenbrödel", but was not able to do so. Herr
Johann Strauss was ill. . . .

For the moment it seemed as if there was no particular
need for anxiety. He improved somewhat, and Professor
Notnagle, his medical man, seemed optimistic. But by the
30th things looked serious. The doctors, called in, became
alarmed. Fever and cough betrayed the fact that he was
suffering from double pueumonia.

The great man was not apprehensive himself. He complained of neuralgia, but was otherwise serene and cheerful.
Then, suddenly, he began to wander in his mind. The
Chinese design on the doors of the stove which served to
heat his room suggested to him dancing figures out of
ballets and operettas, and he became delirious.

Frau Adèle never left his side. She sent for the Pastor
from the Evangelical Church, and the whole house in the
Igelgasse was filled with the gravest foreboding. The
sufferer was restless, and sang and shouted at night. He
rambled about times long past, asked for the score of
"Aschenbrödel", but seldom seemed aware of immediate
things. His malady gained apace, and he had little stamina
left to withstand it.

He came to himself during the morning of the third of June, took his wife's hand in his and kissed it. She said, "Try to sleep a little", and he replied, "I shall do that anyhow!" He died very quietly, without marked suffering, at about a quarter past four in the afternoon of the same day. . . .

When word of his death went forth over the city of Vienna, men could not believe their ears. Vienna without Johann Strauss!!

.   .   .   .   .

Three days later one of the greatest and saddest civic funerals which ever wound its mournful way to the Central Cemetery, called the entire city into the streets. His violin was carried in the great procession, lying on a red velvet cushion. Nothing had been seen like this unending cortège since the death of the poet Grillparzer. It was a beautiful day in early summer.

The houses all along the route were hung with black; tossing plumes on the terrific hearse and an immense concourse of lanterns burning wanly in the sunshine added their own strange note to the sombre scene. The Procession left the house, passed slowly by the mourning Theater-ander-Wien, and paused at the Evangelical Church in the Dorotheagasse. It proceeded, then, past the Opera House to the home of the Music Society of Vienna at whose black-hung portals an oration was held over the dead Master.

They laid the Waltz King to rest near Franz Schubert and Johannes Brahms. They held farewell orations over his grave—orations spoken by the most important men in Vienna—and a Choral Society sang Brahms' "Fahr wohl".

It would serve no purpose further to describe Johann Strauss' elaborate funeral celebrations here. His music, with which we have been chiefly concerned, was now stilled, and with his passing there also passed a period which is not likely to come again. The pre-war world is dreadfully far off now, and those comparatively prosperous and merry decades which our grandfathers knew, both at home and abroad, have utterly sunk below the horizon of time.

On that sad, forgotten day when Johann Strauss was buried in Vienna, the whole laughing, frolicking, dancing city wept. Nothing was heard in the silent, densely packed streets, as the endless procession went slowly by, but the tolling of the bells of innumerable city churches. It was a brazen-tongued wailing which filled the Kaiserstadt: it filled Austria, and went echoing throughout the world.

Johann Strauss, the Waltz King, was dead.

He left behind[1] an immense amount of music, complete and incomplete, much of which has been carefully examined and classified since his death.

The ballet "Aschenbrödel", a modernised version of the old Cinderella fairy tales, was edited and finished by an accomplished musician, Josef Bayer, and produced on the 4th of October, 1908, in the Court Opera House, where all of it recognised as coming from Strauss' own hand was especially applauded. Much of it, necessarily, was pseudo-Strauss, but such a designation should detract in no way from the value of the immense amount of work Herr Bayer had put in to save the Waltz King's last effort from incompletion.

Besides "Aschenbrödel", something more remained of Strauss, a sort of musical curiosity, to which, during his lifetime, he had destined much that he had now left behind him.

[1] Strauss was a rich man. The will which disposed of his estate was the one he made before setting out on his American venture with Frau Jetty. He left a good deal of money to the Society of the Friends of Music instead o˙ to the religious charitable organizations originally destined to receive it—this on account, possibly, of his later change of faith —and bequeathed the rest of his property in houses and musical usufruct to his wife, her daughter and his sisters.

As recently as the spring, Direktor Jauner, of the Karl Theater, had sought an operetta from Strauss, who had written nothing for him since "Methuselah". It was suggested that full use should be made, to this purpose, of many of the dance pieces and numbers the Master had already written—this to relieve him of too great a press of fresh work, and not to overtax his inspiration.

An enormous amount of material was assembled. The publisher Weinberger exerted himself right and left to approach other of Strauss' publishers and obtain their consent to a re-issue, "to bring various pieces together under one hat" as Decsey puts it. The best known and most popular of the Strauss melodies found themselves heaped together with a mass of old forgotten waltzes, polkas and quadrilles, and of unknown things, which the composer himself could have sworn never came from his pen. The sorting of this immense miscellany was a big business in itself, and had occasioned Strauss many surprises. He was raking through the almost wasteful output of a long, vivid, and busy musical lifetime.

Meantime two men, Victor Léon and Leo Stein, wrote the libretto destined to be fitted to this resurrection pie. It was an amusing story of the Vienna Congress period, staged in localities identified with Strauss and his career, with Döbling and Hietzing. A ball, of course, figured in it, and the usual confusion of identities. The usual resulting complications and final clearings up, which seemed to form the stock in trade of anything really destined to make a hit on the lighter boards of Vienna, were the basis of the piece. It was called "Wiener Blut", a title which translates badly, derived from the query "Stärkt Wiener Blut den Mut",—does it make for courage to have Viennese Blood in your veins?

No one can have any idea what gruelling work it was to

put this piece together. The operetta was to be completed by September, libretto, score, instrumentation and all. The collaborators sent out an SOS for assistance.

Then in the May, Strauss fell ill and died!

On his death-bed, he agreed that the help they sought for "Wiener Blut" had best be given by Adolf Müller, a conductor long associated with the orchestra of the Theater-an-der-Wien. Müller, a typical Viennese, and a fully capable musician, accepted the arduous undertaking. The huge box of musical manuscripts and fragments was turned over to him, and he gave himself to the work with the greatest assiduity and most discriminating taste. He was a theatrical expert, and knew all there was to know about the composition and production of operettas. In this case his great aim was to preserve intact the Strauss note and feeling.

Death came to the great composer himself, and Müller brought the operetta to its end. Everyone connected with the Karl Theater had the greatest hopes of it. It was put on with an excellent cast, regardless of expense, nearly six months after Strauss had been in his grave (25th October, 1899.) And it failed. . . .

Most of its numbers were too familiar. So much of it was so well-known beforehand. Jauner was in despair, as much about the public as on his own account. "I can't understand 'em a bit!" he pondered, "They've lost their taste for the best! I just don't know where I am!" His disappointment was so severe it almost led to a breakdown. Strauss' posthumous operetta scarcely ran for a month!

Three years later the management of the Theater-an-der-Wien found themselves in a difficulty owing to a sudden break with Girardi. They hastily put on ' Wiener Blut" to tide it over. And again the amazing thing happened which had so often happened to Strauss creations before— it made an outstanding hit! It had an immense success.

The whole theatrical world suddenly discovered "Wiener Blut", and it went triumphantly forth to conquer the boards all over Austria and Germany, and still further afield. It became a favourite all over the world.

Five other operettas deriving from Strauss and the musical wealth he left behind him were edited and knocked together after the model of "Wiener Blut". They were being produced in various places right up to the outbreak of the Great War (Faschingshochzeit came in 1921), but they did little one way or the other to affect the unique reputation of

JOHANN STRAUSS
THE WALTZ KING.

THE END

INDEX

INDEX

253